YOGA FLOW

FOR

TECH MINDS

CULTIVATING BALANCE AND WELLNESS IN THE DIGITAL AGE

****

Harnessing the Power of Yoga to Enhance Productivity,

Reduce Stress, and Improve Overall Well-being

****

DILIP PATIL

DISCLAIMER

This book provides general information only. The author and publisher are not liable for any harm caused by utilizing or abusing the material.

Before starting any new fitness or wellness program, especially if you have pre-existing medical illnesses or injuries, visit a doctor. The author and publisher are not accountable for accidents or health issues from the recommended practices.

Author's experiences, research, and expertise till publishing. The author and publisher cannot guarantee correctness, completeness, or timeliness.

Listen to your body and avoid stances or workouts that cause pain, discomfort, or damage. Yoga instructors ensure appropriate alignment and safety.

External resources are not endorsed or guaranteed. Assess and verify any indicated resources.

Read this book at your own risk. The author and publisher are not liable for damages caused by using or implementing the information.

DEDICATION

This book is dedicated to my heroes, whose extraordinary accomplishments and unshakable dedication have shown me the way. Your triumph shows the power of determination and greatness. You motivate me to aim higher and never settle. Your advice has helped me manage work and wellness in a digital environment where technology blurs the lines. This book combines yoga's wisdom with tech-unique savvy difficulties to honor your influence. My mentors helped me comprehend yoga's effects on us. Your assistance has helped me calmly manage the fast-paced digital world. I dedicate this book to family, friends, and readers. Its wisdom and practices may help you negotiate the modern world with grace and perseverance. Let's embrace balance and well-being while learning from the past and looking forward.

TABLE OF CONTENTS

Preface	10
Introduction	13
A. Technology's Effects	13
B. Digital age balance and wellbeing	16
Chapter 1: Understanding the Mind-Body Connection	20
1.1 Exploring the mind-body Connection	21
1.2 Yoga's Benefits for Techies	24
1.3 Yoga's Role in Technology Balance	28
Chapter 2: Foundations of Yoga for Tech Minds	32
2.1 Yoga Philosophy and Principles	34
2.1 Relaxing and Focusing Breathing	38
2.3 Asanas for Health	41
Chapter 3: Creating a Personal Yoga Practice	45
3.1 Digital Yoga Studios	46
3.2 Personalizing a Yoga Routine	48
3.3 Yoga for Busy Techies	51
Chapter 4: Technology and Health	56
4.1 Mindful technology usage	57
4.2 Digital Detox and Mindfulness	60
4.3 Tech-driven Balance Strategies	63
Chapter 5: Tech Issues and Yoga	67
5.1 Relaxing Neck and Shoulders	69
5.2 Alleviating Eye Strain and Fatigue	71

5.3	Tech-related Stress Reduction	73
Chapter 6: Mindfulness in Daily Life		76
6.1	Mindful Eating and Nutrition Tips	76
6.2	Mindful movement beyond Yoga	79
6.3	Mindfulness in Relationships	81
Chapter 7: Advanced Yoga for Tech Minds		85
7.1	Advanced Asanas for Strength and Flexibility	85
7.2	Meditation for Focus and Clarity	90
7.3	Digital Yoga Spirituality	93
Chapter 8: Challenges and Consistency		98
8.1	Yoga's Common Challenges	99
8.2	Building Resilience and Perseverance	103
8.3	Sustainable Tech-Yoga Balance	106
Chapter 9: Conclusion		110
9.1	Critical Ideas and Methods	111
9.2	Self-care and Harmony	112
9.3	Digital Lifestyle Balance	114
Appendix: Resources for Tech-Minded Yogis		118
A.	Recommended books and articles	121
B.	Yoga apps and online platforms	126
C.	Yoga studios and retreats with a tech focus	130
Acknowledgment		134
About the Author		136
Can you do me a favor?		138
Discover More		140

Preface

"In the midst of movement and chaos, keep stillness inside of you." - Deepak Chopra.

Yoga's old practice meets the fast-paced, ever-changing modern world, requiring a mix of mindfulness, well-being, and balance. "Yoga Flow for Tech Minds: Cultivating Balance and Wellness in the Digital Age" investigates how yoga may improve tech professionals' lives and help them cope with modern life.

During the COVID-19 epidemic, the globe paused to reassess our priorities and adjust to a new way of life. I worked remotely, had virtual meetings, and was always connected as an IT expert. Digital life offered ease and potential, but it also had its drawbacks.

Amidst the chaos and uncertainty, yoga became my guiding light, offering solace and grounding amidst the storms. It became clear to me that the principles of yoga, with its emphasis on mindfulness, self-care, and holistic well-being, were not only applicable but essential for the tech-minded individuals navigating the digital landscape.

Through this book, I aim to share my journey of discovering and integrating yoga into my life as an IT professional. Drawing upon my experiences, research, and the wisdom of ancient yogic teachings, I hope to provide a roadmap for fellow tech minds to cultivate balance, physical vitality, mental clarity, and emotional well-being.

The practice of yoga extends far beyond the physical postures (asanas). It encompasses breathwork (pranayama), meditation, self-reflection, and conscious living. By embracing these elements, we can harness the power of yoga to counteract the sedentary nature of our work, alleviate stress and burnout, enhance focus and productivity, and foster meaningful connections amidst digital noise.

Software engineers, project managers, and UX designers may use this book for yoga, breathing exercises, guided meditations, and practical recommendations. It promotes overall well-being and offers IT professionals health services. With curiosity, openness, and adaptability, read on. Remember, yoga is a personal path that requires attention and gentle self-compassion to alter our lives genuinely.

This book should inspire, empower, and guide your yoga journey. Let's balance our tech-driven lifestyles with yoga's ancient wisdom in the digital era.

Namaste,

DILIP PATIL

Introduction

"Amid the chaotic digital age, Yoga Flow for Tech Minds offers a sanctuary of balance and wellness, empowering individuals to navigate the challenges of the modern world with mindfulness and resilience."

In today's fast-paced and technology-driven world, feeling overwhelmed and disconnected from our well-being is easy. The constant connectivity, information overload, and sedentary lifestyle associated with the digital age can take a toll on our physical and mental health. However, amidst this chaos, a sanctuary is waiting to be discovered—a path toward balance and wellness. Yoga Flow for Tech Minds: Cultivating Balance and Wellness in the Digital Age is a guiding light in this journey, offering a holistic approach to reclaiming harmony in the modern era. By integrating the ancient wisdom of yoga with the challenges faced by tech-savvy individuals, this book empowers readers to cultivate mindfulness, resilience, and a profound sense of well-being. Let's explore how yoga can be the bridge that connects the digital realm with our inner world, enhancing our lives in the process.

A. Technology's Effects

Technology has profoundly impacted various aspects of our lives, shaping how we work, communicate, access information, and navigate the world. Here are some key impacts of technology on our lives.

- **Communication:** Technology has revolutionized communication, making it faster, more convenient, and more accessible. With the advent of smartphones, social media, and messaging apps, we can instantly connect with people across the globe. Communication barriers have been broken down, enabling us to maintain relationships, collaborate on projects, and share ideas effortlessly.
- **Information and Knowledge:** The internet has democratized access to information and knowledge. With a few clicks, we can explore vast information repositories, learn new skills, and stay updated on global events. This easy access to information has empowered individuals and facilitated self-directed learning, transforming how we acquire knowledge.
- **Work and Productivity:** Technology has reshaped the workplace, enhancing productivity and efficiency. Automation, digital tools, and cloud computing have streamlined business processes and enabled remote work possibilities. Communication and collaboration tools have facilitated seamless teamwork, even across geographical boundaries. However, technology has also created challenges, such as the blurring of

work-life boundaries and the risk of constant availability and digital overload.

- **Health and Medicine:** Technology has revolutionized healthcare, improving diagnoses, treatments, and patient care. Advanced medical devices, telemedicine, electronic health records, and data analysis have transformed the healthcare industry. Wearable devices and health-tracking apps enable individuals to monitor their fitness levels and manage their well-being proactively.

- **Transportation and Travel:** Technology has transformed transportation and travel, making it more efficient, accessible, and convenient. From the invention of automobiles and airplanes to the emergence of ride-sharing services and online travel bookings, technology has opened up new possibilities for exploration and connectivity.

- **Entertainment and Leisure:** Technology has dramatically expanded our entertainment and leisure activities options. Streaming platforms, online gaming, virtual reality experiences, and social media provide many entertainment choices. Technology has also transformed how we consume media, with e-books, podcasts, and digital content replacing traditional formats.

- **Social Impact:** Technology has had a profound social impact, shaping societal norms, behaviors, and relationships. Social media platforms have revolutionized how we connect, share, and express ourselves. They have facilitated social movements, given marginalized communities a voice, and provided advocacy and activism platforms.

While technology brings numerous benefits, it also presents challenges and potential negative impacts. These include privacy concerns, cybersecurity threats, social isolation, sedentary lifestyles, information overload, and the digital divide. It is crucial to strike a balance and adopt a mindful approach to harness the benefits of technology while mitigating its potential drawbacks.

B. Digital age balance and wellbeing

The need for balance and wellness in the digital age arises from the unique challenges posed by our increasingly technology-driven lifestyles. Here are some reasons balance and wellness are essential in the digital age.

- **Digital Overload:** The digital age has brought constant information, notifications, and distractions. We are bombarded with emails, social media updates, news alerts, and endless online content. This constant exposure can lead to information overload, mental fatigue, and a lack of focus. Finding balance and practicing wellness helps us manage our digital consumption, set healthy boundaries, and prioritize our well-being.

- **Sedentary Lifestyle:** Technology has made our life easier but more sedentary. Many works, play and socialize on screens. Sedentary lifestyles can cause obesity, cardiovascular disease, and musculoskeletal diseases. Wellness activities like physical activity and mindful movement can counteract our digital lifestyles.
- **Stress and Mental Health:** The fast-paced, always-on digital world might increase stress and harm mental health. Work stress, social media comparison, and FOMO may all impair our well-being. Mindfulness, meditation, and stress management reduce stress, build mental resilience, and promote emotional well-being.
- **Relationship and Connection:** While technology has made it easier to connect with others, it can also lead to a sense of disconnection and superficial relationships. Spending excessive time on screens can hinder real-life interactions, affect social skills, and contribute to feelings of loneliness and isolation. Balancing our digital interactions with face-to-face connections, nurturing meaningful relationships, and practicing

digital detoxes can enhance our overall connection and well-being.

- **Work-Life Integration:** Technology blurs work-life borders. Many people struggle to unplug, resulting in burnout and lower quality of life. In the digital era, balance requires work-life integration, limits, and self-care. This helps people lead fulfilling personal and professional lives.
- **Mindfulness and Presence:** The digital age can pull us into constant distraction and mindlessness. We may be constantly scrolling, multitasking, and being pulled in different directions. Cultivating balance and wellness involves practicing mindfulness, which allows us to be fully present, engage with our surroundings, and cultivate a deeper connection with ourselves and others.

Finding balance and prioritizing wellness in the digital age is crucial for maintaining physical, mental, and emotional well-being. It enables us to navigate the challenges of the modern world with resilience, focus, and a sense of fulfillment. By consciously integrating wellness practices into our lives, we can reclaim control over our relationship with technology and create a harmonious and sustainable digital lifestyle.

Chapter 1: Understanding the Mind-Body Connection

"The mind and body are not separate entities; they are deeply intertwined, and their harmonious connection is key to overall well-being and balance."

Within our being lies a profound connection between our mind and body—a connection that holds immense power over our well-being. In this chapter, we embark on a journey to explore this intricate relationship and unravel its transformative potential. By recognizing the interplay between our thoughts, emotions, and physical sensations, we can tap into a deeper understanding of ourselves and cultivate a sense of harmony in our tech-driven lives. Let us delve into the profound wisdom of the mind-body connection and discover the transformative impact it can have on our overall well-being.

Tech professional Lisa suffers from sleeplessness, migraines, and exhaustion. She attempted several medical therapies, but her problems continued. Lisa found a mindfulness-based stress reduction program, including yoga, meditation, and mind-body activities. She tried it after being skeptical. Mindfulness and yoga made Lisa aware of her thoughts, emotions, and bodily sensations. She understood that stress and tightness in her neck and shoulders, caused by job demands, caused her headaches.

Lisa's symptoms improved after practicing yoga, breathwork, and mindfulness to reduce stress and tension. This profound shift revealed the unmistakable relationship between her mind and body and the possibilities for healing and well-being.

This shows how the mind-body relationship affects our health. It shows how Lisa's mental and emotional condition affected her physical problems. She found relaxation and balance by recognizing this relationship and implementing mind-body activities. This narrative invites us to investigate the mind-body link and how it might enable brilliant geniuses like Lisa to achieve holistic well-being in the digital era.

The chapter discusses psychoneuroimmunology, stress's impact on the body, and yoga and mindfulness's role in mind-body harmony. Readers are encouraged to increase their awareness of the mind-body link and harness its transformational potential to promote balance, resilience, and overall welfare in their tech-driven lives via practical exercises, guided meditations, and inspiring tales.

1.1 Exploring the mind-body Connection

By engaging in various practices and techniques, tech minds can cultivate a harmonious relationship between their mind and body, enhancing well-being and balance in the digital age. Here are some ways to explore the mind-body connection.

- **Cultivating Body Awareness:** Body awareness is foundational in exploring the mind-body connection. This involves paying attention to physical sensations, movements, and the body's messages. Techniques such as body scans, where attention is consciously directed to different body parts, help deepen body awareness. Engaging in gentle yoga postures (asanas) can also facilitate a connection with the body, encouraging mindful movement and alignment.
- **Mindful Breathing and Meditation:** Practicing mindful breathing and meditation allows tech minds to anchor their awareness in the present moment. Focusing on the breath and observing the sensations that arise can help deepen the mind-body connection. Meditation cultivates a non-judgmental awareness of thoughts, emotions, and bodily sensations, fostering a deeper understanding of their interplay. Mindful breathing exercises and guided meditations can be incorporated into daily routines to foster relaxation, reduce stress, and strengthen the mind-body connection.
- **Yoga as a Mind-Body Practice:** Yoga is a powerful modality for exploring the mind-body

connection. Engaging in a yoga practice, which combines physical postures (asanas), breathwork (pranayama), and meditation, supports the integration of the mind and body. Through yoga, tech minds can develop strength, flexibility, and balance in their physical bodies while cultivating mental clarity and emotional well-being.

- **Self-Reflection and Journaling:** Engaging in self-reflection and journaling can deepen the exploration of the mind-body connection. Reflecting on thoughts, emotions, and physical sensations experienced throughout the day enhances self-awareness. Journaling provides a means to express and process these experiences, enabling a greater understanding of how the mind and body influence each other. Reflective prompts and journaling exercises can be provided in the book to guide tech minds in this exploration.

- **Cultivating Mindfulness in Daily Life:** Beyond formal practices, integrating mindfulness into daily life enhances the mind-body connection. Engaging in activities with real presence and attention, such as mindful eating, walking, or even engaging with technology, fosters a deeper connection to the body's experiences. The chapter offers practical tips and exercises to infuse mindfulness into everyday activities, encouraging tech minds to savor moments, connect with the senses, and tune into the mind-body connection throughout the day.

- **Seeking Support and Guidance**: Exploring the mind-body connection can be a profoundly personal journey, and seeking support and guidance can be beneficial. Tech minds may consider attending yoga classes and mindfulness workshops or seeking the guidance of a qualified teacher or therapist specializing in mind-body practices. Engaging in a supportive community or joining online forums can also provide a space for sharing experiences, gaining insights, and finding inspiration.

By engaging in these practices, tech minds can actively explore the mind-body connection and better understand how their thoughts, emotions, and physical sensations interact. The chapter "Understanding the Mind-Body Connection" in the book "Yoga Flow for Tech Minds: Cultivating Balance and Wellness in the Digital Age" provides the tools, techniques, and guidance necessary to embark on this transformative journey and nurture a harmonious relationship between the mind and body.

1.2 Yoga's Benefits for Techies

Yoga offers numerous benefits for tech minds, often leading busy and digitally focused lives. Incorporating yoga into their routines can help tech minds cultivate balance, well-being, and resilience in the digital age. Here are some specific benefits of yoga for tech minds.

1. **Stress Reduction:** Yoga provides a powerful tool for managing stress, which is prevalent in the tech industry. Through physical postures (asanas), breathwork (pranayama), and meditation, yoga activates the body's relaxation response, reducing stress hormone levels such as cortisol. Regular yoga practice helps tech minds develop effective coping mechanisms and resilience to handle work-related pressures and maintain a sense of calm amidst the demands of the digital world.

2. **Improved Focus and Concentration:** Yoga involves mindful movement and breath awareness, which can enhance concentration and focus. Tech minds often face distractions and information overload, making maintaining attention on a task challenging. Yoga cultivates the ability to anchor attention in the present moment, increasing mental clarity and improving productivity. By integrating yoga into their routine, tech minds can enhance their ability to stay focused and engaged in their work.

3. **Physical Well-being:** Sedentary desk jobs and prolonged screen time can lead to physical ailments such as poor posture, back pain, and muscular

imbalances. Yoga offers a holistic approach to physical well-being, promoting strength, flexibility, and balance. The practice of asanas helps tech minds counteract the effects of a sedentary lifestyle, improve posture, increase body awareness, and prevent or alleviate physical discomfort. Yoga also supports a healthy immune system and improves overall cardiovascular health.

4. **Mental and Emotional Resilience:** The mindfulness aspect of yoga fosters self-awareness and emotional intelligence, enabling tech minds to navigate the ups and downs of the digital world with resilience. By observing thoughts and emotions without judgment during yoga practice, tech minds develop the capacity to respond to challenges with greater clarity and emotional balance. Yoga also helps regulate the nervous system, reducing anxiety and promoting well-being, enhancing mental and emotional resilience.

5. **Better Sleep:** Many tech minds struggle with sleep issues, often due to the overstimulation of screens and a busy mind. Yoga provides techniques to calm the nervous system and promote relaxation, helping tech minds improve the quality of their sleep. By incorporating gentle, restorative yoga poses and relaxation techniques before bedtime,

tech minds can unwind, release tension, and create optimal conditions for a restful night's sleep.

6. **Enhanced Self-Care and Work-Life Integration**: Yoga encourages self-care and self-reflection, which are vital for maintaining a healthy work-life balance. Tech minds often face challenges in setting boundaries and taking time for themselves. Yoga fosters a sense of self-nurturing and self-compassion, reminding tech minds of the importance of prioritizing their well-being. By integrating yoga into their routine, tech minds can create space for self-care, leading to greater overall satisfaction and work-life integration.

7. **Connection and Community:** Yoga allows tech minds to connect with like-minded individuals and build a supportive community. Participating in yoga classes, workshops, or online communities fosters a sense of belonging and offers an avenue for social interaction and support. This connection and community can counteract feelings of isolation from excessive screen time and digital interactions.

By embracing yoga, tech minds can tap into its transformative potential and reap its many benefits. From stress reduction and improved focus to physical well-being and enhanced self-care, yoga empowers tech minds to find balance, wellness, and resilience in the fast-paced and digital world they navigate.

1.3 Yoga's Role in Technology Balance

Yoga can be a powerful tool for balancing the effects of technology in various ways. Here are some detailed explanations of how yoga can help counterbalance the impacts of technology.

- **Physical Balance:** Technology often involves prolonged periods of sitting and repetitive movements, leading to imbalances in the body. Yoga helps restore physical balance by promoting strength, flexibility, and alignment. The practice of asanas (yoga poses) targets different muscle groups, improves posture, and counteracts the sedentary nature of technology use. Regular yoga can alleviate musculoskeletal issues, improve circulation, and enhance physical well-being.
- **Mindful Awareness:** Technology can pull our attention in multiple directions, leading to scattered thoughts and mental overload. Yoga cultivates mindful awareness by bringing attention to the present moment. Through breath-focused movement and meditation, tech minds learn to be fully present and develop a greater capacity to focus and concentrate. This enhanced awareness can help

manage distractions, improve productivity, and reduce mental stress caused by technology.

- **Stress Reduction:** Technology often contributes to increased stress levels, whether due to constant connectivity, information overload, or the pressure to stay connected and productive. Yoga offers effective stress management techniques through deep breathing, relaxation exercises, and activating the parasympathetic nervous system. These practices help reduce stress hormones, promote relaxation, and restore a sense of calm and balance amidst technology demands.

- **Emotional Well-being:** Technology may cause anxiety, restlessness, and detachment. Meditation, breathwork, and mindfulness in yoga promote emotional equilibrium. These techniques improve self-awareness, emotional control, and resilience. Yoga promotes self-compassion, self-care, and emotional well-being.

- **Digital Detox:** Yoga helps techies set limits and take breaks. Yoga lets you unplug from screens and alerts. Tech brains may turn inside by practicing yoga, breathing, and mindfulness. This purposeful disengagement promotes mental clarity, refreshment, and a healthy relationship with technology.

- **Mind-Body Integration:** Technology distracts from physical requirements. Yoga stresses the mind-body connection, fostering overall well-beiBy practicing yoga, tech brains may reconnect with their bodies, improve body awareness, and acknowledge bodily feelings practicing yoga. Mind-body integration promotes self-awareness and equilibrium.
- **Self-Reflection and Intention Setting:** Yoga encourages self-reflection and introspection, growing tech minds to examine their relationship with technology. Through practices like journaling, meditation, and setting intentions, yoga helps tech minds develop a mindful and intentional approach to technology use. This self-reflection can lead to a more balanced and conscious engagement with technology, ensuring it serves as a tool rather than a source of overwhelm or distraction.

By incorporating yoga into their lives, tech minds can counterbalance the effects of technology and cultivate a sense of balance, well-being, and mindfulness. Through physical movement, breathwork, mindful awareness, and self-reflection, yoga empowers individuals to develop a healthier relationship with technology, supporting their overall physical, mental, and emotional health.

Chapter 2: Foundations of Yoga for Tech Minds

"Yoga is the journey of the self, through the self, to the self." - The Bhagavad Gita.

In today's fast-paced, digitally connected world, where screens dominate our lives, and stress seems an ever-present companion, it has become increasingly vital for tech minds to find balance and wellness. The relentless pursuit of innovation and the demands of the tech industry can often leave us mentally and physically drained. In this context, the ancient practice of yoga emerges as a beacon of hope, offering a path toward reclaiming harmony amidst the chaos.

Maya is a skilled software developer at a top IT business. Maya's colleagues admired her coding skills. However, back-to-back meetings, tight deadlines, and continuous alerts filled her days. Her brain raced with knowledge, and her body ached from long hours crouched over a computer.

As Maya's stress levels rose, she noticed their toll on her well-being. She experienced frequent headaches, restless nights, and a lingering sense of dissatisfaction. In search of a solution, she stumbled upon an article about the transformative power of yoga for tech professionals. Intrigued, Maya decided to try it, attending her first yoga class with a mix of curiosity and skepticism.

From the moment Maya stepped onto her mat, something shifted within her. As she followed the teacher's gentle guidance, her breath synchronized with her movements, creating a sense of rhythm and presence she had not felt in years. Gradually, the outside world faded away, and Maya found herself immersed in the sensations of her own body, discovering an oasis of tranquillity amidst the chaos.

Through consistent practice, Maya discovered that yoga was not just about physical postures or flexibility; it was a holistic system that nurtured the mind, body, and spirit. She learned to navigate the intricate dance between effort and surrender, finding the delicate balance between pushing her limits and listening to her body's wisdom. As she delved deeper into the teachings of yoga, Maya began to uncover the profound connections between her inner landscape and her work as a tech professional.

With time, Maya noticed that her mind became sharper and more focused, allowing her to approach complex coding challenges with clarity and creativity. She discovered that the moments of stillness and introspection cultivated on her mat had a ripple effect, leading to heightened productivity and a newfound capacity to navigate stress with grace. Yoga became essential in her tech toolkit; We empower her to thrive in the digital age while maintaining her well-being.

Maya's journey is just one example of the transformative power of yoga for tech minds. In this chapter, we will explore the foundations of yoga, demystifying its ancient wisdom and providing practical tools specifically tailored for those immersed in the world of technology. Together, we will embark on a path of self-discovery, cultivating balance and wellness amid the digital whirlwind. Get ready to flow, breathe, and reconnect with the essence of who you indeed are.

2.1 Yoga Philosophy and Principles

Yoga philosophy encompasses a rich and ancient tradition that originated in ancient India. It is a comprehensive system that addresses various aspects of human existence, including physical, mental, emotional, and spiritual well-being. Yoga philosophy guides how to lead a balanced and fulfilling life by integrating body, mind, and spirit. Here are some fundamental principles and concepts of yoga philosophy.

- **The Eight Limbs of Yoga (Ashtanga):** The foundation of yoga philosophy is based on the teachings of Patanjali's Yoga Sutras, which outline the eight limbs of yoga. These limbs serve as a roadmap for personal transformation and self-realization. They are.
    1. **Yamas (ethical restraints)**: These moral principles guide our behavior towards others

and include non-violence, truthfulness, non-stealing, continence, and non-greed.
2. **Niyamas (observances)**: These personal practices promote self-discipline and include cleanliness, contentment, self-study, self-discipline, and surrender to a higher power.
3. **Asanas (physical postures)**: These are the physical poses practiced in yoga, which help develop strength, flexibility, balance, and awareness.
4. **Pranayama (breath control)**: Pranayama involves various breathing techniques that enhance the flow of life force energy (prana) in the body, promoting vitality and relaxation.
5. **Pratyahara (withdrawal of senses)**: Pratyahara refers to turning inward and withdrawing attention from external stimuli, allowing one to focus on the inner realm of consciousness.
6. **Dharana (concentration)**: Dharana involves developing focused concentration on a single object or point, such as the breath or a mantra, to achieve a state of mental stillness.
7. **Dhyana (meditation)**: Dhyana is the practice of sustained meditation, where the mind becomes calm and focused, leading to expanded awareness and tranquility.

8. **Samadhi (blissful absorption):** Samadhi is the ultimate goal of yoga, representing a state of complete union and transcendence. It is a state of profound joy, inner peace, and oneness with the universe.

- **Union of Body, Mind, and Spirit:** Yoga philosophy emphasizes the integration and harmony of the body, mind, and spirit. It recognizes that these aspects are interconnected and that true well-being arises from their alignment and unity. Yoga seeks to create balance and integration within the individual through asanas, pranayama, and meditation.

- **The Law of Karma:** Karma is a fundamental principle in yoga philosophy, which states that every action has consequences. It emphasizes that we are responsible for our choices and actions, and these choices shape our present circumstances and future experiences. One can create positive karma and promote personal growth and spiritual evolution by cultivating positive intentions and actions.

- **The Concept of Dharma:** Dharma refers to one's righteous duty or path in life. It is aligned with one's true nature and purpose, and living by dharma brings fulfillment and harmony. Yoga philosophy encourages individuals to discover their unique dharma and live authentically, contributing to the greater good of society.

- **Non-Attachment (Vairagya):** Yoga philosophy emphasizes the practice of non-attachment, recognizing that attachment to desires and outcomes leads to suffering. By cultivating a state of non-attachment, one can find inner freedom and contentment, regardless of external circumstances.
- **Self-Realization:** Yoga philosophy views self-realization or self-discovery as the ultimate goal of human existence. It involves transcending the limited identification with the ego and connecting with one's true essence, often referred to as the self or Atman. Self-realization brings a deep sense of fulfillment, inner peace, and understanding of the interconnectedness of all beings.

These principles and concepts of yoga philosophy provide a framework for living a balanced and meaningful life. They encourage self-awareness, self-discipline, compassion, and spiritual growth, ultimately leading to greater well-being and a sense of connection with the world around us.

2.1 Relaxing and Focusing Breathing

Breathing techniques are an essential aspect of yoga and are used to enhance relaxation and focus. In the fast-paced world of technology, where stress and distractions are every days, mastering these techniques can significantly benefit tech minds. This chapter will explore various breathing techniques for relaxation and focus and their contradictions.

1. **Diaphragmatic Breathing:** Diaphragmatic breathing, also known as belly or deep breathing, is a total relaxation and stress reduction technique. It involves engaging the diaphragm, a dome-shaped muscle beneath the lungs, to draw air deep into the lungs. This technique promotes a state of calm and activates the body's relaxation response. **Contradiction** - There are no significant contradictions associated with diaphragmatic breathing. However, individuals with certain respiratory conditions, such as chronic obstructive pulmonary disease (COPD), may find it challenging to perform this technique. Such individuals should consult with a healthcare professional before practicing diaphragmatic breathing.

2. **Alternate Nostril Breathing:** Alternate nostril breathing is a powerful technique for balancing and calming the mind. It involves gently closing one nostril while inhaling through the other, switching nostrils, and exhaling through the opposite side. This technique helps synchronize the left and right hemispheres of the brain, promoting mental clarity

and focus. **Contradiction** - Alternate nostril breathing is generally safe for most individuals. However, it may not be suitable for those with nasal congestion or blockages, as it requires clear nasal passages to perform effectively. Additionally, individuals with high blood pressure should exercise caution and consult a healthcare professional before practicing this technique.

3. **Box Breathing:** Box breathing, also known as square breathing, is a technique that involves equalizing the length of each breath to create a sense of balance and focus. It consists of a four-step process: inhaling for a specific count, holding the breath, exhaling for the exact count, and holding the breath again before starting the cycle anew. This technique is beneficial for reducing anxiety and enhancing concentration. **Contradiction** - Box breathing is generally safe for most individuals. However, individuals with respiratory conditions or a history of dizziness or fainting should approach this technique cautiously. If any discomfort or adverse effects occur during the practice, it is advisable to discontinue and consult with a healthcare professional.

4. **Kapalabhati**: Kapalabhati, also known as skull-shining breath, is an energizing breathing technique that cleanses the respiratory system and

invigorates the mind. It involves short, forceful exhales generated by powerful contractions of the lower belly, followed by passive inhales. This technique increases oxygen supply, stimulates the abdominal organs, and enhances mental alertness. **Contradiction** - individuals with heart conditions, high blood pressure, hernias, or abdominal discomfort or injury should avoid Kapalabhati. It is essential to practice this technique under the guidance of an experienced yoga teacher to ensure proper technique and avoid any potential contradictions.

5. **Ujjayi Breathing**: Ujjayi breathing, often referred to as victorious breath, is a technique that involves slight constriction of the throat during both inhalation and exhalation. This creates an audible ocean-like sound and helps focus the mind. Ujjayi breathing promotes deep relaxation and concentration and can enhance stability during asana (posture) practice. **Contradiction** - Ujjayi breathing is generally safe for most individuals. However, individuals with respiratory conditions, such as asthma, or those prone to dizziness, should practice this technique with caution. If any discomfort arises, it is advisable to discontinue the practice and consult a healthcare professional.

Breathing techniques are valuable tools for tech minds seeking relaxation and focus amid a technology-driven lifestyle. However, it is essential to understand the contradictions associated with each technique and exercise caution, especially if you have pre-existing respiratory conditions or medical concerns. Consulting with a healthcare professional or an experienced yoga teacher can provide personalized guidance and ensure safe practice.

2.3 Asanas for Health

In today's fast-paced world, where stress and sedentary lifestyles have become the norm, finding ways to achieve physical and mental well-being is paramount. One powerful tool that has withstood the test of time is the practice of postures, or asanas, which form an integral part of various disciplines like yoga and mindfulness. These postures, carefully designed to engage the body and mind in a harmonious union, offer a multitude of benefits for both our physical and mental health. By incorporating specific poses into our daily routine, we can unlock a world of improved flexibility, strength, balance, and inner peace. Whether you're a beginner seeking to embark on a journey of self-discovery or an experienced practitioner looking to deepen your practice, exploring the realm of asanas can be a transformative experience, guiding you toward holistic well-being.

Asanas for Physical Well-being

1. **Mountain Pose (Tadasana):** Stand tall with your feet hip-width apart, shoulders relaxed, and arms by your sides. This posture helps improve posture, strengthens the legs, and promotes balance and stability. This posture is consistent.
2. **Chair Pose (Utkatasana):** Begin by standing with your feet together. Inhale and raise your arms overhead, palms facing each other. Exhale and bend your knees as if sitting back in an imaginary chair. This posture strengthens the lower body, tones the leg muscles, and improves stability. People with knee injuries or low blood pressure should avoid this posture.
3. **Tree Pose (Vrikshasana):** Start by standing with your feet hip-width apart. Shift your weight onto your left foot and place the sole of your right foot on your left inner thigh. Bring your hands to your heart center or extend them overhead. Tree pose improves balance, strengthens the legs, and enhances concentration. Individuals with ankle or hip injuries should avoid this posture.
4. **Downward Facing Dog (Adho Mukha Svanasana):** Begin on your hands and knees. Exhale and lift your knees away from the floor, straightening your legs and raising your hips towards the ceiling. This posture stretches the entire body, particularly the hamstrings and

shoulders while energizing the mind. People with wrist or shoulder injuries should avoid this posture.

Asanas for Mental Well-being

1. **Child's Pose (Balasana):** Start kneeling on the floor. Bring your buttocks towards your heels and lower your torso between your thighs. Extend your arms forward or relax them alongside your body. The child's pose helps release back, shoulders, and neck tension, promoting relaxation and calming the mind. Individuals with knee injuries or digestive issues should avoid it.

2. **Corpse Pose (Savasana):** Lie on your back with your legs extended, arms relaxed alongside your body, and palms facing up. Close your eyes and allow your body to relax completely. Savasana promotes deep relaxation, reduces stress, and helps restore energy levels. This posture is consistent.

3. **Bridge Pose (Setu Bandhasana):** Lie on your back with your knees bent and feet hip-width apart. Inhale, press your feet into the ground, and lift your hips, creating a bridge shape with your body. This posture strengthens the back, opens the chest, and relieves stress and anxiety. People with neck or shoulder injuries should avoid this posture.

4. **Cat-Cow Pose (Marjaryasana-Bitilasana):** Begin on your hands and knees in a tabletop

position. Inhale, arch your back, lift your head, and look up (Cow Pose). Exhale, round your spine, tuck your chin to your chest and draw your belly in (Cat Pose). This dynamic movement improves spinal flexibility, releases tension, and brings focus to the breath. Individuals with wrist or back injuries should avoid this posture.

Incorporating these foundational asanas into a tech-minded individual's daily routine can profoundly impact physical and mental well-being. However, listening to your body, respecting its limits, and consulting with a qualified yoga instructor if you have any specific medical conditions or concerns is essential. Remember that yoga is not solely about physical postures but also about cultivating mindfulness, breath awareness, and finding balance in all aspects of life.

Chapter 3: Creating a Personal Yoga Practice

"Yoga is not about touching your toes; it's about what you learn on the way down." - Judith Hanson Lasater.

In the hustle and bustle of the tech-driven world, finding a sense of balance and inner peace can often feel like an elusive goal. However, amidst the chaos, yoga emerges as a powerful tool to reconnect with oneself and cultivate a sense of mindfulness. In this chapter, we delve into creating a personal yoga practice tailored specifically for individuals navigating the demands of the digital age. By understanding the fundamental principles and exploring practical strategies, you will embark on a transformative journey toward integrating yoga into your daily life. Through a thoughtful blend of ancient wisdom and modern insights, this chapter guides you to develop a sustainable and enriching yoga practice that harmonizes with your tech-driven lifestyle.

Software developer Sarah types code on her PC. Deadlines, bug fixes, and email inboxes fill her head. Her fast-paced profession makes her emotionally exhausted, physically tight, and alienated from her body. Sarah wants a method to relax and take care of herself despite the stress. "Yoga Flow for Tech Minds" intrigues her, and she excitedly goes to Chapter 3 to see how she may integrate yoga into her tech-driven existence.

3.1 Digital Yoga Studios

Setting up a yoga space in the digital age for tech minds can be a great way to combine the benefits of technology with the practice of yoga. Here's a step-by-step guide to help you set up your digital yoga space.

- **Choose a Dedicated Space:** Select a quiet and comfortable area in your home where you can practice yoga without distractions. It could be a spare room, a corner of your living room, or a section of your bedroom.

- **Declutter and Organize:** Clear the chosen space of any clutter or unnecessary items. Please keep it clean and free from distractions. Consider adding some plants or natural elements to create a soothing ambiance.

- **Set Up Your Yoga Mat:** Invest in a high-quality yoga mat that suits your needs. Tech minds may prefer mats that integrate with smart devices or offer additional features such as tracking your yoga sessions or providing real-time feedback on your postures.

- **Arrange for Tech Integration:** If you enjoy using technology during your yoga practice, set up a dedicated area for your devices. This could include a tablet or a laptop for accessing online yoga classes, a smartphone for yoga apps, or a smart TV for streaming yoga videos. Ensure you have a stable internet connection in your yoga space.

- **Install a Sound System:** Consider adding a sound system or speakers to enhance your yoga experience. You can play soothing music, ambient sounds, or guided meditation during your practice. Bluetooth or intelligent speakers can be connected wirelessly to your devices for easy control.
- **Lighting and Ambiance:** Pay attention to the lighting in your yoga space. Natural light is ideal, but choose soft and warm lighting options if impossible. Avoid harsh or bright lights that may hinder relaxation. Intelligent lighting systems like Philips Hue can be controlled with your devices, allowing you to create the perfect ambiance for your practice.
- **Create Storage Solutions:** Organize yoga props and accessories like blocks, straps, bolsters, or blankets. Invest in storage solutions like shelves or baskets to keep them neatly organized and easily accessible.
- **Personalize the Space:** Add personal touches to make the space feel inviting and inspiring. You can

hang motivational quotes or artwork related to yoga, place a small altar or statue, or use essential oils or incense for aromatherapy.

- **Online Access Resources:** Take advantage of the vast online yoga resources. Subscribe to reputable yoga platforms or YouTube channels that offer a variety of classes and styles. Explore apps that provide guided yoga sessions or meditation practices.
- **Set Boundaries:** As a tech-minded individual, it's essential to set boundaries to prevent distractions during your yoga practice. Turn off notifications on your devices, set specific practice times, and communicate your boundaries with family or roommates.

Remember, while technology can enhance your yoga practice, finding a balance and remaining present is crucial. Allow your digital yoga space to be a sanctuary where you can disconnect from the digital world and reconnect with your mind, body, and breath.

3.2 Personalizing a Yoga Routine

Designing a personalized yoga routine for tech minds involves considering their unique needs and challenges. Here's a step-by-step guide to help you create a yoga routine tailored for individuals in the tech industry.

- **Assess individual needs:** Understand the specific requirements of the tech minds you're designing the routine for. Consider factors such as their typical posture, tension or stiffness, stress levels, and any specific goals they have in mind (e.g., improving flexibility, reducing back pain, increasing focus).
- **Start with breath awareness:** Tech minds often spend long hours sitting and staring at screens, which can lead to shallow breathing and reduced oxygen intake. Begin the routine with a few minutes of breath awareness exercises, such as deep belly breathing or alternate nostril breathing. This helps to calm the mind and bring attention to the present moment.
- **Incorporate gentle warm-up exercises:** Since tech minds often sit for extended periods, it's essential to warm up the body before diving into deeper yoga postures. Include gentle movements like neck rolls, shoulder rolls, wrist and ankle rotations, and seated spinal twists to mobilize the significant joints and release tension.
- **Address common tech-related issues:** Many tech professionals experience neck and shoulder pain, lower back stiffness, and tight hips. Integrate poses that target these areas, such as seated neck

stretches, shoulder openers (e.g., Eagle Arms), forward folds, cat-cow stretches, and hip-opening poses like Pigeon Pose or Butterfly Pose.

- **Focus on posture correction:** Sitting for extended periods often leads to poor posture. Include yoga postures that promote good posture and strengthen the core and back muscles. Poses like Mountain Pose, Cobra Pose, Bridge Pose, and Locust Pose can help improve spinal alignment and build postural awareness.

- **Enhance focus and concentration:** The tech industry requires intense mental focus, so include yoga practices that boost concentration. Poses like Tree Pose, Warrior III, and Eagle Pose challenge balance and concentration. Meditation techniques, such as mindfulness or focusing on a single point (Trataka), can also be beneficial.

- **Integrate stress reduction techniques:** Tech minds often experience high-stress levels. Incorporate relaxation and stress reduction practices into the routine. Include restorative poses like Child's Pose, Legs-Up-The-Wall Pose, and Savasana (Corpse Pose). Please encourage them to practice mindfulness or guided relaxation during these poses to promote mental and emotional relaxation.

- **Keep it manageable and adaptable:** Make sure the routine is realistic and adaptable to different schedules. Tech professionals often have limited time, so design a routine that can be completed within 20-30 minutes if necessary. Please encourage them to practice consistently and gradually increase the duration or intensity as they progress.
- **Encourage regular breaks:** Alongside the personalized yoga routine, advise tech minds to take regular breaks from prolonged sitting. Please encourage them to incorporate short movement breaks, such as stretching or walking, throughout their workday to combat the adverse effects of prolonged sitting.

Remember, it's essential to consult with individuals to understand their unique needs, limitations, and any existing medical conditions before designing a personalized yoga routine. Consider collaborating with a qualified yoga instructor or therapist to ensure safety and effectiveness.

3.3 Yoga for Busy Techies

Integrating yoga into a busy tech lifestyle can benefit your physical and mental well-being. While the fast-paced nature of the tech industry often leads to stress, long hours of sitting, and mental fatigue, incorporating yoga practices can help counterbalance these effects and promote a healthier lifestyle. Here's a detailed guide on integrating yoga into a busy tech lifestyle.

- **Recognize the Benefits:** Understanding the advantages of yoga can motivate you to make it a part of your routine. Yoga offers physical benefits such as increased flexibility, improved posture, and enhanced strength. Additionally, it promotes mental well-being, reduces stress, and improves focus and concentration.
- **Start with Short Sessions:** As a tech professional, time is often limited. Begin by allocating short periods, such as 10-15 minutes, for yoga practice. You can gradually increase the duration as you become more comfortable and see the benefits.
- **Establish a Routine:** Consistency is critical. Identify a time slot that works best for you, whether in the morning, during a lunch break, or in the evening. Set a regular schedule for your yoga practice to make it easier to integrate into your daily routine.
- **Create a Dedicated Space:** Designate a specific area in your home or office to practice yoga without distractions. Having a dedicated space helps create

a conducive environment and encourages regular practice.

- **Choose the Right Style:** Yoga encompasses various styles, so explore options to find what resonates with you. For busy tech professionals, styles like Hatha, Vinyasa, or Yin yoga can be beneficial. These styles offer a balance of physical movement, stretching, and relaxation.
- **Utilize Technology:** Leverage technology to your advantage. There are numerous yoga apps, online videos, and podcasts available that provide guided yoga sessions. These resources allow you to practice yoga anytime, anywhere, making it convenient for your tech lifestyle.
- **Incorporate Yoga during Breaks:** Take short yoga breaks throughout your workday. Perform a few stretches, deep breathing exercises, or quick standing poses to release tension and rejuvenate your body and mind.
- **Practice Mindfulness and Meditation:** Yoga goes beyond poses. Practice awareness and meditation. These routines can relax, focus, and reduce stress. Use apps or classes to learn meditation techniques.
- **Join Yoga Communities:** Engage with like-minded individuals by joining yoga communities or

attending yoga classes. Participating in group sessions provides a supportive environment, offers motivation, and helps you stay committed to your yoga practice.
- **Explore Chair Yoga:** Tech professionals often sit at desks. Try chair yoga. These seated yoga positions offset the consequences of extended sitting.
- **Practice Breath Awareness:** Pay attention to your breath throughout the day. Incorporate deep breathing exercises, such as "box breathing" or "4-7-8 breathing," to reduce stress and increase oxygen flow to the brain. These techniques can be practiced discreetly during work hours.
- **Prioritize Self-Care**: Make self-care a priority. Alongside yoga, ensure you get enough sleep, maintain a balanced diet, and take breaks to relax and recharge. Integrating yoga into your busy tech lifestyle should be part of an overall holistic approach to well-being.

Remember, yoga demands dedication and consistency. Begin slowly and patiently. Yoga will improve your physical and mental health, helping you succeed in tech while staying balanced.

Chapter 4: Technology and Health

"Technology is a useful servant but a dangerous master."
Christian Lous Lange.

In this chapter, the author delves deep into the intricate interplay between technology and our well-being, emphasizing the importance of maintaining a balanced and mindful approach toward our digital lives. The chapter explores the profound impact of technology on our physical, mental, and emotional health, highlighting the potential pitfalls and offering invaluable guidance on fostering a harmonious connection with the digital world. To empower individuals to find serenity amidst the digital chaos, the author introduces practical techniques and yoga-inspired practices to navigate the ever-evolving landscape of technology. By encouraging readers to cultivate self-awareness, set boundaries, and practice conscious consumption, the chapter equips tech minds with the necessary tools to reclaim control over their relationship with technology. It serves as a beacon of wisdom, reminding us that a mindful approach towards technology can enhance our well-being, deepen our connections, and ultimately lead us towards a more balanced and fulfilling life.

As I mentioned in an earlier chapter, the story of Sarah, a dedicated software engineer who found herself constantly overwhelmed by the demands of her tech-driven career.

Despite her passion for innovation and the positive impact she desired to make, Sarah struggled with burnout and an unhealthy attachment to her devices. Through the teachings and practices outlined in the chapter, Sarah learned to integrate mindfulness into her daily routine. She discovered the power of setting digital boundaries, designating tech-free zones in her home, and implementing regular technology detoxes. As a result, Sarah experienced a profound shift in her well-being, gaining a sense of calm and clarity that had previously eluded her. With her newfound balance, she could navigate the demands of her career with greater ease, nurturing her physical and mental health along the way. Sarah's story is an inspiring example of how adopting a mindful approach toward technology can transform our relationship, leading to a healthier and more fulfilling life.

4.1 Mindful technology usage

Mindful technology usage refers to the conscious and intentional use of technology to support well-being, productivity, and overall mental health. It involves developing awareness and engaging with technology to promote balance, reduce stress, and foster a healthy relationship with digital devices. For tech minds, who often spend significant time working with technology, incorporating mindful practices into their tech usage can be particularly beneficial. Here are some critical aspects of mindful technology usage for tech minds:

- **Intentional device usage:** Tech minds can start by setting clear intentions for their device usage. Before using a device, they can ask themselves questions like: "What specific tasks do I want to accomplish?", "How much time do I need?" and "What is my purpose for using this device?" This helps in avoiding mindless browsing or excessive time spent on unproductive activities.
- **Setting boundaries:** Tech minds must establish boundaries around technology usage. This can include allocating specific time slots for work, leisure, and rest and sticking to those time limits. Additionally, setting boundaries around notifications and establishing "tech-free" zones or times, such as during meals or before bed, can promote better focus and work-life balance.
- **Digital decluttering:** Regularly decluttering digital spaces, such as email inboxes, desktops, and app folders, can help reduce digital overwhelm and create a more organized and efficient digital environment. Tech minds can apply principles like "inbox zero" to manage emails effectively, uninstall unnecessary apps, and logically organize files.

- **Mindful breaks:** It is crucial for maintaining focus and avoiding burnout. Tech minds can incorporate short breaks into their work routine, during which they step away from the screen, stretch, practice deep breathing exercises, or engage in activities that promote relaxation and rejuvenation. These breaks allow the mind to recharge and can enhance productivity and well-being.
- **Mindful consumption:** Being mindful of the content consumed online is essential for mental well-being. Tech minds can critically evaluate the quality and relevance of the information they encounter, fact-check sources, and seek diverse perspectives. They can also curate their digital feeds by following accounts that provide meaningful and inspiring content, fostering positive emotions and personal growth.
- **Digital mindfulness tools:** Numerous apps and tools are available to support mindful technology usage. For example, meditation and mindfulness apps can help tech minds practice mindfulness and reduce stress. Productivity apps can assist in time management and task organization. Screen time tracking apps can provide insights into device usage patterns and help identify areas for improvement.

Experimenting with different tools and finding ones that align with personal preferences can be beneficial.

- **Reflection and self-awareness:** Regular reflection on one's technology usage habits and their impact on well-being is essential to mindful technology usage. Tech minds can periodically assess their digital habits, noting any areas of concern or imbalance. This self-awareness helps make conscious choices about technology usage and adapt behaviors accordingly.

By incorporating these practices, tech minds can develop a healthier relationship with technology, maintain focus, enhance productivity, and promote overall well-being. Mindful technology usage allows individuals to harness the benefits of technology while minimizing its potential negative impacts on mental health and work-life balance.

4.2 Digital Detox and Mindfulness

Digital Detox is when individuals intentionally disconnect from digital devices and online activities to reduce reliance on technology and create a healthier life balance. It involves taking a break from constant connectivity and consciously setting aside time to focus on other activities that promote well-being and mindfulness. Here are some key aspects and practices related to Digital Detox and mindfulness for tech minds.

- **Understanding the Need for Digital Detox:** In today's digital age, people are often immersed in constant information and distractions from their electronic devices. This can lead to decreased productivity, increased stress levels, sleep disturbances, and a decreased ability to be fully present in real-life interactions. Recognizing the negative impact of excessive technology use is the first step toward implementing a digital detox.
- **Setting Boundaries:** Establishing clear boundaries for technology use is crucial. This involves defining specific times and places where devices will not be used, such as during meals, before bed, or social gatherings. Individuals can reclaim their time and attention for other meaningful activities by creating these boundaries.
- **Creating Device-Free Zones:** Designating certain areas or rooms in your living space as device-free zones can help you detach from technology. For example, the bedroom can be designated a device-free zone to improve sleep quality and create a peaceful environment. Similarly, having technology-free zones during family time or meals can enhance personal connections and communication.

- **Unplugging from Social Media:** Social media platforms are known for their addictive nature and the potential to consume excessive amounts of time. Consider taking a break from social media by deactivating accounts temporarily or using apps that limit your usage. This break can help reduce comparison, anxiety, and the fear of missing out (FOMO).
- **Engaging in Mindful Practices:** Mindfulness intentionally brings attention to the present moment without judgment. Incorporating mindfulness techniques into your daily routine can help cultivate a healthier relationship with technology. Some practices include:

1. **Meditation**: Set aside a few minutes daily to sit quietly, focus on your breath, and observe your thoughts and sensations. Meditation helps calm the mind, reduce stress, and increase self-awareness.
2. **Deep Breathing:** When you feel overwhelmed or distracted by technology, take a moment to pause and take several deep breaths. This simple practice helps bring you back to the present moment and promotes relaxation.
3. **Mindful Eating:** Practice mindful eating rather than eating while scrolling through your phone or working on the computer. Pay attention to the tastes, textures, and smells of your food. Chew

slowly and savor each bite, allowing yourself to experience the meal entirely.

4. **Nature Walks:** Spending time in nature can be a great way to disconnect from technology and reconnect with the natural world. Take a walk in a park or forest, and pay attention to the sights, sounds, and sensations around you.

- **Engaging in Offline Hobbies:** Explore activities that do not involve technology to fill the void left by digital detox. This could include reading physical books, engaging in art or crafts, playing musical instruments, exercising, or spending quality time with loved ones. Find activities that bring you joy and allow you to be fully present in the moment.

Remember that digital detox and mindfulness practices are highly individualized. It's essential to experiment and find what works best for you. Gradually incorporating these practices into your routine can lead to a healthier relationship with technology and improved overall well-being.

4.3 Tech-driven Balance Strategies

In a tech-driven world, finding balance can be a significant challenge for individuals who are deeply involved in the tech industry or have tech-oriented minds. The relentless pace of technological advancements, the constant connectivity, and the digital age demands can lead to imbalances in various aspects of life. However, there are several strategies that tech minds can employ to find balance and maintain their well-being. Here are some key strategies.

- **Set clear boundaries:** Establish boundaries between work and personal life. Define specific working hours and try to stick to them. Avoid checking work emails or engaging in work-related activities during personal time. This helps create separation and allows for time to relax and recharge.
- **Prioritize self-care:** Take care of your physical, mental, and emotional well-being. Regularly exercise, get sufficient sleep, and maintain a healthy diet. Allocate time for activities that bring you joy and help you unwind, such as hobbies, spending time with loved ones, or pursuing non-tech interests.
- **Practice mindful technology use:** Be mindful of your technology usage and its impact on your well-being. Take regular breaks from screens, practice digital detoxes, and limit social media consumption. Engage in activities that promote mindfulness, such as meditation or deep breathing exercises, to reduce stress and improve focus.

- **Foster real-world connections:** Balance tech-focused interactions with meaningful, in-person connections. Engage in social activities, join clubs or groups related to your non-tech interests, and spend quality time with family and friends. Building solid relationships offline helps counterbalance the isolation from excessive tech use.
- **Continuously learn and explore:** While staying up-to-date with technological advancements is essential, don't limit your learning solely to tech-related topics. Explore other areas of interest, such as art, literature, philosophy, or nature. This broadens your perspective, stimulates creativity, and offers new growth and personal development avenues.
- **Seek work-life integration:** Instead of strict work-life separation, aim for work-life integration. Identify ways to align your tech-driven work with your values and interests. Look for opportunities to use technology to enhance your personal life and well-being, such as productivity tools or wellness apps.
- **Establish digital boundaries:** Define limits on your digital engagement. Designate specific time blocks where you disconnect from devices and

create tech-free zones in your home. This allows for mental and emotional space, reduces information overload, and encourages more meaningful offline experiences.
- **Delegate and seek support:** Recognize that you can't do everything alone. Delegate tasks, collaborate with others, and seek support when needed. This helps alleviate the pressure and allows you to focus on the areas requiring your attention.
- **Embrace work-life flexibility:** Explore flexible work arrangements, such as remote work or flexible hours. This provides more control over your schedule and enables a better work-life balance.
- **Reflect and reassess regularly:** Reflect on your priorities, values, and goals. Regularly reassess your work-life balance and make necessary adjustments. Be open to adapting your strategies as your circumstances and priorities change.

Remember, finding balance is a personal journey, and the strategies that work for one person may differ from another. It's essential to experiment, learn from your experiences, and adjust accordingly to create a sustainable and fulfilling balance in a tech-driven world.

Chapter 5: Tech Issues and Yoga

'The human spirit must prevail over technology.' - Albert Einstein,

Technology is a double-edged sword that has revolutionized our lives, enabling us to connect, create, and explore like never before. However, as we immerse ourselves deeper into the digital realm, we often encounter various physical and mental challenges. The constant use of screens, sedentary lifestyles, and information overload can take a toll on our bodies and minds.

In this chapter, we embark on a journey to discover the transformative power of yoga in addressing these common tech-related issues. As skilled programmer writes elegant code, we aim to cultivate a mindful flow that can debug our physical discomforts, declutter our minds, and restore balance in our tech-driven lives.

Software engineer Maya was young. She lived in a bustling metropolis. She spent hours bent over her computer creating and fixing complex computer systems. Her dedication to her profession drove Maya's sudden climb to prominence, but it cost her. As she got increasingly tech-dependent, she started having issues.

Maya's eyes were tired after hours of screen time. Poor posture and lengthy sitting gave her tension headaches and a stiff neck. Information inundated her mind, causing worry, anxiety, and difficulty focusing.

Maya tried yoga to transform. She joined a yoga class for tech-challenged people to bring balance and well-being to her tech-filled existence. She didn't realize this would ease her physical pain and change her technological connection.

Candlelight welcomed Maya to her mat for the first time. The knowledgeable and experienced yoga instructor started class by saying, *"Center yourself in technology's cacophony. Discover quiet in digital noise."* These remarks and Albert Einstein inspired Maya.

Maya studied tech-related yoga postures in class. She relieved her tired eyes with gentle stretches and thoughtful motions, gaining clarity and vision. She felt lighter and more relaxed after doing neck and shoulder asanas.

Yoga took Maya inside. Each breath allowed her to settle her mind. Meditation and mindfulness helped her calm her mind. Maya achieved equilibrium on and off the mat as she tuned into her body and mind.

Maya included yoga in her regular regimen after her transformation. She gracefully handled her tech-driven existence with greater power, flexibility, and mental resilience. Yoga became her haven from technology, allowing her to reset and reconnect with herself.

5.1 Relaxing Neck and Shoulders

While yoga can be a powerful tool for relieving neck and shoulder tension, it is essential to practice with awareness and consider any contraindications or limitations you may have. Here are some yoga practices that can help alleviate tension in the neck and shoulders, along with their contraindications.

- **Neck Rolls:** Sit or stand comfortably with a straight spine. Gently drop your chin towards your chest and slowly roll your head in a circular motion, moving from side to side. This movement should be done cautiously if you have neck injuries or conditions like cervical spondylosis. If you experience pain or discomfort, avoid rolling the neck and focus on gentle stretching and mobility exercises.

- **Eagle Arms:** Sit or stand tall and extend your arms straight in front of you. Cross your right arm over the left, bend your elbows, and bring your palms to touch if possible. This pose is contraindicated for individuals with shoulder injuries, such as rotator cuff tears or impingement. If you have shoulder issues, avoiding this pose or modifying it by placing the back of your hands together is best.

- **Cow Face Pose (Gomukhasana) Arms:** Sit cross-legged or on a chair with your spine tall. Extend your right arm straight towards the ceiling and bend it, reaching your right hand behind your neck. Simultaneously, bend your left arm straight to the side, sliding your left hand up your back. This pose may not be suitable for individuals with shoulder, neck, or upper back injuries or limited range of motion. Modify the pose using a strap or towel to bridge the gap between your hands, or work on gentle shoulder stretches without interlacing the fingers.
- **Thread the Needle:** Begin on all fours in a tabletop position. Extend your right arm straight before you, then slide it under your left arm, bringing your right shoulder and cheek to the mat. This pose should be avoided if you have shoulder or neck injuries or experience pain or discomfort while performing it. Instead, focus on gentle shoulder stretches or opt for supported variations that provide more stability and support.
- **Supported Fish Pose:** Sit on the edge of a folded blanket or bolster. Lie back, allowing the prop to support your upper back and head while keeping your lower back on the ground. This pose may not be suitable for individuals with neck injuries,

cervical spine issues, or difficulty lying flat on their backs. If you have any concerns or limitations, it is best to consult with a healthcare professional or experienced yoga instructor for guidance on appropriate modifications or alternative poses.

Remember, it's crucial to honor your body's limitations and practice yoga mindfully, especially when dealing with contraindications. If you have specific concerns or conditions, seeking guidance from a qualified yoga instructor who can provide personalized modifications and ensure your practice is safe and beneficial for your needs is recommended.

5.2 Alleviating Eye Strain and Fatigue

Eye strain and fatigue are common issues experienced by individuals who spend long hours working on computers and staring at screens. Yoga offers practices that can help alleviate these symptoms and promote eye health. However, it's essential to practice with awareness and consider any contraindications or limitations you may have. Here are some yoga practices to alleviate eye strain and fatigue and their contraindications.

- **Palming:** Sit comfortably with your eyes closed. Rub your palms together vigorously until they become warm. Cup your palms and place them gently over your closed eyes, allowing the warmth and darkness to soothe your eyes. Breathe deeply and relax. This practice is generally safe for everyone and can be done regularly to relieve eye strain.

- **Eye Exercises:** Sit comfortably with a straight spine. Start by moving your eyes in different directions - up and down, side to side, diagonally. Then, rotate your eyes clockwise and counterclockwise. These eye exercises can help improve blood circulation and reduce eye strain. However, it is best to consult an eye specialist before practicing these exercises if you have any eye conditions or recent eye surgeries.

- **Trataka (Candle Gazing):** Sit comfortably with a lit candle at eye level, about arm's length away. Gently gaze at the flame without blinking for as long as comfortable. This practice helps improve focus and strengthen eye muscles. However, if you have sensitive eyes, eye infections, or any retinal issues, it is advisable to avoid Trataka or perform it under the guidance of an experienced yoga teacher.

- **Eye Massage:** Gently massage your closed eyes in circular motions using your fingertips. Apply gentle pressure around the eye sockets, temples, and brow bone area. This can help relieve tension and increase circulation around the eyes. Avoid pressing

too hard or rubbing vigorously, especially if you have eye conditions, injuries, or infections.
- **Eye Exercises with Blinking:** Sit comfortably and relax your face. Open your eyes wide, then slowly blink 10-15 times, ensuring a complete blink with each repetition. This exercise helps to lubricate the eyes and prevent dryness and strain. It is generally safe for most individuals, but consult an eye specialist if you have any specific eye conditions before practicing.

Remember to listen to your body and be aware of discomfort or pain during these practices. Suppose you have any pre-existing eye conditions, recent eye surgeries, or concerns about your eye health. In that case, it is advisable to consult with an eye specialist or healthcare professional before incorporating these practices into your routine. They can provide personalized guidance and recommendations based on your needs and ensure that the practices are safe and suitable.

5.3 Tech-related Stress Reduction

Stress and anxiety are familiar companions of our tech-driven lives, but yoga offers a holistic approach to finding relief and restoring balance to the mind. It's essential to practice yoga with awareness and consider any contraindications or limitations you may have. Here are some yoga practices to ease stress and anxiety associated with technology, along with their contraindications.

- **Mindful Breathing:** Find a comfortable seated position, close your eyes, and bring your attention to your breath. Take slow, deep breaths, focusing on the sensation of the breath entering and leaving your body. If you have any respiratory conditions or difficulties with breath control, modify the practice by taking gentle, natural breaths without forceful or prolonged breath retention.
- **Gentle Yoga Asanas:** Practice gentle yoga poses that promote relaxation and release tension. Examples include the Child's Pose (Balasana), Legs-Up-The-Wall Pose (Viparita Karani), and Corpse Pose (Savasana). If you have any injuries, limitations, or concerns related to your physical health, modify or avoid poses that may exacerbate those conditions. Listening to your body and practicing within your comfortable range of motion is essential.
- **Meditation:** Find a quiet space and sit comfortably. You can choose a meditation technique that resonates with you, such as mindfulness meditation or loving-kindness meditation. However, suppose you have any mental health conditions or difficulties with meditation

practices. In that case, it's advisable to consult with a mental health professional or experienced meditation teacher for guidance tailored to your needs.

- **Digital Detox:** Take intentional breaks from technology to recharge and reset your mind. During these breaks, engage in activities that bring you joy and help you disconnect, such as spending time in nature, practicing hobbies, or connecting with loved ones. Setting boundaries around technology usage can also reduce the stress and anxiety associated with it.
- **Yoga Nidra:** Practice Yoga, also known as yogic sleep, is a guided relaxation technique that helps calm the nervous system and reduce anxiety. However, if you have any sleep disorders or concerns related to relaxation practices, consult a healthcare professional or experienced yoga teacher to ensure they suit you.

Everyone's needs and limitations are unique, so honoring your body and mind throughout your yoga practice is essential. If you have specific concerns or conditions, you should seek guidance from a qualified yoga instructor, mental health professional, or healthcare provider who can provide personalized modifications, techniques, and support based on your needs.

Chapter 6: Mindfulness in Daily Life

"You can't stop the waves, but you can learn to surf" - Jon Kabat-Zinn.

As we delve deeper into the captivating chapter on mindfulness in daily life, we are introduced to the inspiring story of Sarah, a highly accomplished computer professional. Sarah's narrative unfolds as she stumbles upon the transformative power of mindfulness amidst the relentless pressures and demands of her work. Through Sarah's enlightening journey, we gain invaluable insight into the profound impact that mindfulness can have on our overall well-being. This chapter serves as a guide, illuminating the path toward cultivating a more profound sense of presence, equilibrium, and resilience by incorporating mindfulness into our daily routines. We invite you to embark on this exploration with us as we uncover practical techniques and expert advice to integrate mindfulness into the lives of technology-minded individuals seamlessly. These invaluable practices will empower us to navigate the ever-changing tides of technology with grace and inner tranquility.

6.1 Mindful Eating and Nutrition Tips

In the fast-paced world of tech, where time is often at a premium, cultivating mindful eating habits becomes even more crucial. Mindful eating is a practice that invites tech minds to slow down, engage their senses, and develop a deeper connection with the food they consume. It promotes healthier eating habits, enhances well-being, and supports mental clarity.

For tech minds looking to incorporate mindful eating into their daily lives, here are some detailed nutrition tips and strategies:

1. **Pause and Tune in**: Before you begin your meal or snack, take a moment to pause and tune in to your body. Check your hunger levels, noticing if you're starving or eating out of habit or stress. Mindful eating involves being present and making conscious choices.
2. **Engage Your Senses:** As you eat, engage all your senses to experience the food thoroughly. Observe the colors, textures, and aromas of your meal. Chew slowly and savor each bite, allowing the flavors to unfold. By engaging your senses, you bring a heightened awareness to eating.
3. **Practice Portion Control:** Mindful eating includes being mindful of portion sizes. Pay attention to the fullness signals and stop eating when you feel satisfied rather than overly full. This practice can help maintain a healthy weight and prevent overeating.

4. **Choose Nutrient-Dense Foods:** In tech, relying on quick, processed foods is easy. However, prioritizing nutrient-dense options is crucial for optimal well-being. Incorporate a variety of fruits, vegetables, whole grains, lean proteins, and healthy fats into your meals. These foods provide essential nutrients and energy for your busy lifestyle.
5. **Mindful Snacking:** Snacking is common among tech professionals. Instead of mindlessly munching on snacks, take a moment to pause and consider if you're starving. Opt for nourishing snacks like fresh fruits, nuts, or yogurt, and savor them mindfully.
6. **Minimize Distractions:** Technology often accompanies mealtime, leading to mindless eating. Minimize distractions by putting away devices and creating a dedicated space for meals. Please focus on the food in front of you, fostering a sense of gratitude for the nourishment it provides.
7. **Meal Planning and Preparation:** With busy schedules, planning and preparing meals in advance can help foster mindful eating habits. Set aside weekly time to plan your meals, create a shopping list, and prepare ingredients. This practice reduces reliance on unhealthy convenience foods and allows you to make mindful choices.
8. **Hydration:** Stay mindful of your hydration throughout the day. Opt for water or herbal teas,

and limit sugary beverages. Staying properly hydrated supports overall well-being and helps maintain focus and clarity.

Remember, cultivating mindful eating habits is a gradual process. Start by incorporating one or two tips at a time and build upon them as you become more comfortable. By nourishing your body with awareness and intention, you can support your well-being as a tech professional and enhance your overall quality of life.

6.2 Mindful movement beyond Yoga

The mindful movement goes beyond yoga and offers tech minds diverse practices to cultivate physical and mental well-being. In the digital age, where sedentary work and screen time are prevalent, incorporating mindful movement into daily routines becomes essential for maintaining a healthy balance. Here are some mindful movement practices beyond yoga that are particularly beneficial for tech minds:

1. **Walking Meditation:** Engage in mindful walking to connect with the present moment and experience the sensations of each step. Focus on the movement of your feet, the rhythm of your breath, and the sights and sounds around you. Walking meditation provides a refreshing break from screens while promoting physical activity and mental clarity.

2. **Tai Chi:** Embrace the ancient Chinese practice of Tai Chi, which combines flowing movements, deep breathing, and mindfulness. This martial art form helps improve balance, flexibility, and posture while promoting a sense of calm and relaxation. Practicing Tai Chi can counteract the effects of prolonged sitting and enhance overall well-being.

3. **Mindful Stretching:** Incorporate mindful stretching breaks throughout the day to release tension and improve flexibility. Pay attention to your body's sensations and move with intention, focusing on the stretched muscles. This practice promotes physical well-being and brings awareness to your body-mind connection.

4. **Desk Yoga:** Incorporate mini yoga sequences or stretches into your workday to counteract the sedentary nature of desk-bound tasks. Simple neck stretches, shoulder rolls, and seated twists can help release tension and promote circulation. Desk yoga provides an opportunity to reconnect with your body and alleviate stiffness.

5. **Mindful Dance:** Engage in free-form or guided dance sessions to express yourself and experience the joy of movement. Allow the music to guide you, tuning into your body's natural rhythms and sensations. Dancing mindfully provides a creative

outlet and can be a fun and energizing way to release stress and tension.

6. **Mindful Breathing Exercises:** Focus on your breath as a central anchor for mindfulness during physical activity. Incorporate deep, intentional breathing to bring your attention to the present moment and promote relaxation. Breathing exercises can be practiced during any movement, whether walking, stretching, or engaging in other forms of exercise.

Remember, the key to mindful movement is to bring a sense of presence, awareness, and intention to the activity. Find practices that resonate with you and fit into your schedule, allowing you to reconnect with your body, clear your mind, and find balance amid technology-driven demands. By incorporating mindful movement into your daily life, you can nurture your physical and mental well-being as a tech professional.

6.3 Mindfulness in Relationships

Practicing mindfulness in interpersonal relationships is particularly valuable for tech minds who often navigate high-pressure work environments and rely heavily on digital communication. By cultivating mindfulness in their interactions with others, tech professionals can enhance the quality of their relationships, improve communication, and foster a sense of connection and empathy. Here are some key aspects of practicing mindfulness in interpersonal relationships:

- **Active Listening:** Mindful communication starts with active listening. When engaging in conversations, give your full attention to the person speaking. Set aside distractions like devices or internal thoughts, and listen with an open mind and heart. Be present, show genuine interest, and avoid interrupting or jumping to conclusions. This practice fosters a deeper understanding and promotes meaningful connections.
- **Non-judgmental Awareness:** Cultivate non-judgmental awareness in your interactions. Instead of making assumptions or forming preconceived notions about others, approach each interaction with curiosity and openness. Allow thoughts and judgments to arise without attaching to them, and strive to see things from different perspectives. You create a space for authentic and compassionate communication by embracing non-judgmental awareness.
- **Emotional Intelligence:** Develop emotional intelligence by being attuned to your own emotions and those of others. Notice your emotional responses during interactions and strive to regulate them mindfully. Similarly, practice empathy by

recognizing and validating the emotions of others. This heightened emotional awareness allows for more empathetic and meaningful connections.

- **Mindful Speech:** Mindful speech involves choosing words intentionally and speaking with kindness and compassion. Before speaking, pause and reflect on the impact of your words. Use language that is respectful, considerate, and clear. Avoid unnecessary criticism, sarcasm, or defensive responses. Mindful speech fosters understanding, diffuses conflicts, and nurtures healthy communication dynamics.

- **Presence in Virtual Communication:** Practicing mindfulness in virtual communication is vital in an increasingly digital world. Be aware of the tone and intention behind your written messages. Take the time to read and reflect on your words before sending them. Avoid impulsive or reactive responses, and be mindful of the potential for misinterpretation in text-based communication. Strive to cultivate authentic and meaningful connections even through digital platforms.

- **Setting Boundaries:** Mindfulness in interpersonal relationships also involves setting healthy boundaries. Recognize your limits and communicate them respectfully. Be mindful of the boundaries of others and respect their need for space and personal time. Setting and honoring boundaries promotes healthier and more balanced relationships.

- **Conflict Resolution:** When conflicts arise, approach them with mindfulness. Step back to observe your thoughts, emotions, and physical sensations before engaging in conflict resolution. Practice active listening, empathetic communication, and non-reactivity. Seek solutions that are mutually beneficial and promote understanding rather than escalating tensions. Mindful conflict resolution fosters harmony and cooperation.

Mindfulness in relationships improves communication, strengthens bonds, and creates a friendly workplace. Mindfulness takes effort and self-reflection. Tech thinkers may improve their professional and personal connections with these abilities.

Chapter 7: Advanced Yoga for Tech Minds

"Yoga is not just repetition of few postures; it is more about the exploration and discovery of the subtle energies of life." - Amit Ray.

Steve Jobs, the visionary co-founder of Apple Inc., was not only known for his revolutionary contributions to technology but also his deep understanding of the importance of inner balance. Despite his busy and demanding schedule, Jobs recognized the need to cultivate a calm and focused mind to navigate the ever-evolving tech landscape. He once shared his experience of finding solace and renewed clarity through yoga. Jobs acknowledged that the ancient art of yoga offered invaluable tools for tech minds to harmonize their thoughts, increase self-awareness, and enhance overall well-being.

7.1 Advanced Asanas for Strength and Flexibility

Advanced asanas for strength and flexibility for tech minds are a set of challenging yoga poses that focus on developing physical strength, flexibility, and overall body awareness. These poses are specifically curated for individuals who work in the tech industry and may spend prolonged periods sitting or engaging in repetitive movements. By incorporating advanced asanas into their yoga practice, tech minds can counterbalance the effects of their sedentary work lifestyle and improve their physical well-being. Here are some advanced asanas (yoga poses) for strength and flexibility, along with contraindications and guidance on how to approach them for tech minds:

- **Utthita Hasta Padangusthasana (Extended Hand-to-Big-Toe Pose):** This pose helps enhance strength, balance, and flexibility. However, a common contraindication for tech minds is tight hip flexors due to prolonged sitting. To approach this pose safely, begin with gentle hip-opening exercises such as lunges or low lunges to warm up the hip flexors. You can also use a strap or belt to hold the lifted leg if reaching the toe is challenging. Focus on engaging the core and maintaining proper alignment while gradually working towards straightening the leg.
- **Ardha Chandrasana (Half Moon Pose):** Ardha Chandrasana improves strength, concentration, and body coordination. Individuals with balance issues or dizziness should take precautions when attempting this pose. Start with practicing near a wall or with a chair for support. Gradually work on developing core strength and stability to improve balance. Engage the standing leg and keep the gaze focused on a fixed point to help maintain balance. A qualified yoga instructor

can provide guidance on modifications and tips for finding stability in this pose.

- **Ustrasana (Camel Pose):** Ustrasana helps improve posture, spine flexibility, and core strength. However, tech minds who experience neck or lower back issues should exercise caution. Begin with gentle backbends to warm up the spine before attempting Ustrasana. Keep the hands on the lower back or use blocks for support to avoid strain. Engage the core and lengthen the tailbone towards the floor to protect the lower back. If neck discomfort arises, keep the gaze forward or slightly downward rather than tilting the head back.

- **Pincha Mayurasana (Forearm Stand):** Pincha Mayurasana strengthens the upper body, improves balance, and increases focus. However, individuals with shoulder or wrist injuries or instability should avoid or modify this pose. Strengthen the shoulders and wrists gradually with preparatory exercises such as Dolphin Pose. Use a wall for support when practicing the pose initially. Ensure the forearms are parallel and the weight is evenly distributed. Seek guidance from a yoga instructor to ensure proper alignment and modifications.

- **Hanumanasana (Monkey Pose):** Hanumanasana is an advanced split pose that enhances flexibility, stamina, and mental focus. Tech minds with tight hamstrings or hip issues should approach this pose mindfully. Prioritize warming the hamstrings and hips with gentle stretches and preparatory poses like lunges and wide-legged forward folds. Use props such as blocks or blankets for support if needed. Avoid forcing the split and focus on gradually increasing flexibility over time. Regular practice and patience will contribute to progress in this pose.

- **Eka Pada Rajakapotasana (One-Legged King Pigeon Pose):** This pose helps open the hips, stretch the quadriceps, and increase spinal flexibility. However, individuals with knee or hip injuries should approach this pose with caution. Begin in a low lunge position, bring one knee forward, and place it on the mat just behind the wrist. Extend the opposite leg back, keeping the hips square. Slowly lower the upper body down and rest on the forearms or forehead. Avoid any pain or discomfort and modify the pose if needed.
- **Bakasana (Crow Pose):** Bakasana is an arm balance that strengthens the arms, wrists, and core while improving balance and focus. Individuals with wrist or shoulder issues should practice this pose mindfully. Start in a squatting position with the feet hip-width apart. Place the hands firmly on

the ground, shoulder-width apart. Lean forward and place the knees on the upper arms. Shift the weight forward and engage the core. Lift the feet off the ground, finding balance in the hands. Practice against a wall or use blocks for support if necessary.

- **Natarajasana (Lord of the Dance Pose):** Natarajasana is a standing balance pose that improves strength, balance, and flexibility. It also opens the shoulders and stretches the quadriceps. Individuals with balance or hip issues should take caution when attempting this pose. Begin in a standing position and shift the weight onto one foot. Bend the opposite knee and reach back to hold the inner ankle or foot. Extend the opposite arm forward for balance. Slowly kick the foot into the hand, lifting the leg while leaning slightly forward. Maintain a steady gaze and engage the core for stability.

- **Vrischikasana (Scorpion Pose):** Vrischikasana is an advanced inversion that strengthens the shoulders, core, and arms while improving balance and focus. However, individuals with neck, shoulder, or back issues should avoid this pose. Begin in a forearm stand position against a wall. Slowly walk the feet up the wall while lifting the hips higher. Bend the knees and allow the feet to fall over the head, reaching for the ground. Engage

> the core and balance the weight evenly on the forearms. Use the wall for support and practice under the guidance of an experienced instructor.

Remember to approach advanced asanas mindfully, respecting your body's limitations and avoiding pain or discomfort. Always warm up properly, listen to your body, and seek guidance from a qualified yoga instructor who can provide personalized modifications and help you progress safely. Building strength and flexibility gradually is vital to enjoying the benefits of these advanced poses while minimizing the risk of injury.

7.2 Meditation for Focus and Clarity

Meditation is a practice that involves focusing the mind and cultivating a state of inner calm and clarity. It has been used for centuries to promote relaxation, reduce stress, and enhance mental well-being. Meditation can be valuable for tech minds seeking enhanced focus and clarity. Here's an in-depth explanation of meditation, its techniques, contradictions, and steps to practice it effectively:

Meditation Techniques

  a. **Mindfulness Meditation:** This technique involves paying attention to the present moment without judgment. It entails focusing on the breath, bodily sensations, thoughts, or external stimuli. The goal is to observe these experiences without getting caught up in them, fostering a sense of presence and awareness.

b. **Loving-Kindness Meditation:** Also known as Metta meditation, this technique involves cultivating feelings of love, compassion, and goodwill towards oneself and others. It typically involves silently repeating phrases of well-wishes and directing them towards oneself, loved ones, neutral individuals, and even difficult people.

c. **Concentration Meditation:** This technique focuses on a single focus point, such as the breath, a mantra, a candle flame, or a specific image. The aim is to develop sustained concentration and mental stability.

Contradictions in Meditation for Tech Minds: While meditation can offer numerous benefits, there are a few contradictions for tech minds.

a. **Restless Mind**: Tech minds often have busy and active minds due to work demands. It can be challenging for them to settle into a meditative state, as the mind may resist the stillness and calmness required. Patience and perseverance are necessary to overcome this contradiction.

b. **Impatience:** Tech minds may seek instant results and quick solutions. Meditation is a practice that requires consistent effort and time to yield noticeable benefits. It is essential to approach meditation with a long-term perspective and embrace the process rather than focusing solely on immediate outcomes.

c. **Overstimulation:** Constant exposure to technology and digital devices can lead to sensory overload and overstimulation. It may be beneficial for tech minds to find a quiet and calm environment for meditation to counterbalance the high-stimulus nature of their work.

Steps to Practice Meditation for Enhanced Focus and Clarity

1. Find a quiet, comfortable space to sit or lie down without distractions.
2. Close your eyes or soften your gaze, allowing yourself to relax and settle into the present moment.
3. Choose a meditation technique that resonates with you, such as mindfulness or concentration meditation.
4. Set an intention for your practice to enhance focus and clarity.
5. Begin by taking a few deep breaths, allowing your body and mind to relax.

6. Please direct your attention to your chosen focus point, whether it's your breath, a mantra, or bodily sensations.
7. As thoughts arise, observe them without judgment and gently bring your focus back to the present moment.
8. Practice for a predetermined duration, starting with a few minutes and gradually increasing the time as you become more comfortable.
9. After the practice, take a moment to reflect on any insights or experiences that arose during meditation.
10. Consistency is critical. Aim to practice meditation daily, even briefly, to establish a routine and experience the cumulative benefits.

By incorporating regular meditation into their routine, tech minds can cultivate enhanced focus and clarity. However, it's important to approach meditation with an open mind, be patient with the process, and adapt the practice to suit individual needs and preferences. With time and consistent effort, meditation can become a valuable tool for promoting mental well-being and achieving a more transparent, focused state of mind.

7.3 Digital Yoga Spirituality

Exploring the spiritual aspects of yoga in the digital age can be a transformative journey for tech minds seeking a deeper connection with themselves and the world around them. While technology has undoubtedly revolutionized our lives, it has also created a fast-paced and often disconnected environment. With its ancient roots and spiritual foundations, yoga offers tech minds an opportunity to find balance, meaning, and a sense of inner fulfillment. Here's an in-depth explanation of exploring the spiritual aspects of yoga for tech minds in the digital age.

Understanding the Spiritual Aspects of Yoga:

a. **Union of Mind, Body, and Spirit:** Yoga, at its core, is a holistic practice that aims to unite the mind, body, and spirit. It goes beyond the physical postures (asanas) and incorporates breathwork (pranayama), meditation, ethical principles (yamas and niyamas), and self-reflection to facilitate personal growth and spiritual awakening.

b. **Cultivating Self-Awareness:** The spiritual aspect of yoga encourages tech minds to delve inward and develop a deeper understanding of themselves. Through mindful movement, breath awareness, and meditation, they can observe their thoughts, emotions, and behavior patterns, gaining insights into their true nature and fostering self-acceptance.

c. **Connection with Something Greater:** Yoga invites tech minds to explore their connection with something greater than themselves, whether it's referred to as the divine, universal consciousness, or simply a sense of interconnectedness with all beings. This connection can provide a profound sense of purpose, belonging, and a broader perspective on life.

Navigating the Digital Age Mindfully:

a. **Creating Digital Boundaries:** Tech minds are often immersed in the digital world, leading to overstimulation and detachment from the present moment. Setting boundaries around technology use, such as designated tech-free times or digital detoxes, allows space for introspection and spiritual exploration.

b. **Utilizing Technology Mindfully:** While technology can be a distraction, it can also be a powerful tool for spiritual growth. Tech minds can leverage apps, online courses, and guided meditations to support their yoga and spiritual practices. They can use technology to connect with like-minded communities, access spiritual teachings, and deepen their understanding of spiritual traditions.

c. **Integrating Yoga and Mindfulness into Daily Life:** The digital age often promotes multitasking and constant busyness. Tech minds can counterbalance this by integrating yoga and mindfulness into their daily lives. This includes mindful eating, mindful communication, taking regular breaks for stretching and breathwork, and finding moments of stillness amidst the fast-paced nature of technology.

Exploring Yogic Philosophies and Traditions

a. **Studying Yogic Texts:** Tech minds can dive into ancient yogic texts, such as the Yoga Sutras of Patanjali, Bhagavad Gita, or Upanishads, to gain insights into the philosophical underpinnings of yoga. These texts offer profound wisdom on self-realization, ethical living, and the nature of consciousness.

b. **Engaging in Self-Inquiry:** Self-inquiry practices, such as journaling, contemplation, and introspection, can help tech minds explore their beliefs, values, and the more profound questions of life. Reflecting on their experiences on and off the mat fosters self-awareness, personal growth, and spiritual development.

c. **Embracing Rituals and Ceremony:** Rituals and ceremonies have been integral to spiritual practices for centuries. Tech minds can incorporate rituals into their yoga practice, such as lighting a candle, setting intentions, or practicing gratitude.

These rituals create sacred space and offer a sense of reverence and connection.

Seeking Guidance and Community

a. **Finding a Spiritual Teacher:** For tech minds embarking on a spiritual journey, finding a knowledgeable and experienced spiritual teacher or guru can provide guidance, support, and a deeper understanding of yogic principles. A teacher can offer personalized practices, answer questions, and inspire growth.

b. **Connecting with Like-Minded Community:** Engaging with a community of fellow seekers can be invaluable in the digital age. Tech minds can join online forums, attend yoga retreats or workshops, or participate in virtual Satsang (spiritual gatherings) to connect with others on the path and share insights and experiences.

Exploring the spiritual aspects of yoga in the digital age is an invitation for tech minds to find balance, meaning, and a more profound sense of connection within themselves and the world. By cultivating self-awareness, setting digital boundaries, studying yogic philosophies, and seeking guidance, tech minds can embark on a transformative journey that harmonizes their tech-driven lives with their spiritual well-being.

Chapter 8: Challenges and Consistency

'The only way to make sense of change is to plunge into it, move with it, and join the dance.' - Alan Watts.

Sarah is a dedicated tech professional with a passion for innovation and problem-solving. Sarah spends long hours in front of a computer screen, navigating complex coding projects and troubleshooting technical issues. Her work is demanding, requiring her to adapt to rapid changes and tight deadlines. While Sarah thrives in the fast-paced tech world, she often faces challenges that affect her well-being and consistency in maintaining a healthy work-life balance. She notices the toll it takes on her physical health, mental focus, and overall calmness. Realizing the need for a sustainable solution, Sarah turns to yoga. This chapter is dedicated to tech minds like Sarah, who understand the importance of navigating the challenges that arise in their demanding careers while maintaining consistency in their yoga practice. It offers practical guidance, strategies, and insights to help them find equilibrium, overcome obstacles, and stay committed to their well-being amidst the ever-changing tech industry landscape.

In this chapter, tech minds like Sarah are acknowledged for their unique experiences and challenges in the tech industry. The quote by Alan Watts sets the tone for embracing change and adaptability as essential aspects of navigating the tech world. The story of Sarah represents the experiences of many tech professionals who recognize the need for a balanced and consistent approach to maintain their well-being. The chapter promises to provide practical tools and guidance to help tech minds overcome obstacles and find consistency in their yoga practice, enabling them to thrive professionally and personally.

8.1 Yoga's Common Challenges

Common obstacles to yoga practice for tech minds can arise due to the demands and lifestyle of the tech industry. Here are some common obstacles and strategies to overcome them.

Time Constraints: Tech professionals often have demanding schedules and limited free time, which makes it challenging to find time for yoga practice. To overcome this obstacle:

  a. **Prioritize self-care:** Recognize the importance of self-care and make it a non-negotiable part of your routine. Understand that taking care of your physical and mental well-being will ultimately enhance your productivity and overall quality of life.
  b. **Set a regular practice time:** Dedicate a specific time each day for yoga, even if it's just 15-20 minutes. Consistency is vital, and having a set time helps establish a habit. Consider waking up a bit

earlier or incorporating yoga into your evening routine.

c. **Break it down:** If finding an extended period for a complete yoga session feels overwhelming, break it down into shorter sessions throughout the day. Even a few minutes of deep breathing or gentle stretching can make a difference.

Sedentary Lifestyle: Many tech professionals spend extended periods sitting at desks, leading to stiffness, muscular imbalances, and lack of mobility. To overcome this obstacle:

a. **Incorporate desk yoga:** Integrate simple stretches, neck and shoulder rolls, and seated twists into your work routine. These can be done right at your desk and help release tension and increase blood flow.

b. **Take breaks:** Set reminders to take short movement breaks throughout the day. Use these breaks to stand up, walk around, and perform quick yoga poses like forward folds, lunges, or spinal twists to counteract the effects of prolonged sitting.

c. **Practice active yoga styles:** Engage in dynamic and energizing yoga styles like Vinyasa or Power Yoga that incorporate flowing movements and strength-building postures. These practices help counterbalance the sedentary nature of your work and promote mobility and vitality.

Mental Overload and Stress: The tech industry can be mentally demanding, leading to stress and mental fatigue. To overcome this obstacle.

    a. **Use yoga as a stress reliever:** Dedicate time for gentle yoga or restorative practices focusing on relaxation and stress reduction. Incorporate deep breathing exercises, such as alternate nostril breathing or extended exhalations, to activate the body's relaxation response.

    b. **Practice mindfulness:** Incorporate mindfulness meditation into your routine to develop present-moment awareness and reduce stress. Set aside a few minutes daily to sit quietly and observe your thoughts and sensations without judgment.

    c. **Set boundaries:** Establish clear boundaries between work and personal life to create space for relaxation and rejuvenation. Avoid checking emails or engaging in work-related activities during designated personal time, allowing yourself to disconnect and unwind.

Lack of Motivation and Consistency: Maintaining a regular yoga practice can be challenging when motivation wanes. To overcome this obstacle.

a. **Set realistic goals:** Start with small, achievable goals to build momentum and gradually increase the intensity and duration of your practice. Celebrate milestones along the way to stay motivated.
b. **Find accountability:** Partner with a yoga buddy or join a yoga community, in-person or online, to stay motivated and accountable. Share your goals, progress, and challenges with others who can offer support and encouragement.
c. **Vary your routine:** Explore different styles of yoga, attend workshops, or try new online classes to keep your practice fresh and exciting. Experiment with different sequences, props, or meditation techniques to stay engaged and avoid monotony.

Digital Distractions: Tech minds are constantly surrounded by digital devices, which can distract from the present moment and disrupt focus. To overcome this obstacle.

a. **Create a tech-free zone:** Designate a specific area in your home as a yoga sanctuary, free from digital distractions. Keep your yoga mat, props, and any inspiring objects in this space to cultivate a peaceful and focused environment.
b. **Set boundaries with technology:** Establish specific times or durations when you disconnect

from technology and fully engage in your yoga practice. Silence notifications, put your phone on airplane mode, or use apps to block distracting websites during practice.

c. **Use technology mindfully:** While technology can be a distraction, it can also be a valuable tool for supporting your yoga practice. Utilize online resources, yoga apps, or virtual classes purposefully and intentionally without allowing them to dominate your practice time.

Overcoming these obstacles requires commitment, self-awareness, and adaptability. It's essential to approach your yoga practice with compassion and patience, understanding that progress may come in small increments. By finding strategies that work for you and integrating yoga into your tech-driven lifestyle, you can overcome these obstacles and experience the transformative benefits of a consistent yoga practice.

8.2 Building Resilience and Perseverance

Building resilience and perseverance is crucial for tech minds, as technology often involves facing complex challenges, rapid changes, and demanding work environments. Here are some detailed strategies to help tech professionals develop resilience and perseverance.

- **Develop a Growth Mindset:** Embrace a growth mindset, which is the belief that abilities and intelligence can be developed through dedication and hard work. Emphasize learning from failures and setbacks as opportunities for growth rather than seeing them as personal shortcomings.
- **Set Realistic Goals:** Set specific, achievable goals that align with your long-term aspirations. Break down larger goals into smaller, manageable tasks. Celebrate your progress along the way to maintain motivation and build confidence.
- **Cultivate Self-Compassion:** Treat yourself with kindness and understanding, especially when facing challenges or setbacks. Acknowledge that everyone makes mistakes and encounters difficulties. Practice self-compassion by speaking to yourself in a supportive and encouraging manner.
- **Build a Supportive Network:** Surround yourself with a network of colleagues, mentors, and friends who understand the demands of the tech industry. Seek advice, feedback, and emotional support from this network. Collaboration and shared experiences can help you persevere during tough times.
- **Learn from Failures:** Embrace failure as an opportunity for growth and learning. Analyze the

reasons behind failures or setbacks and identify lessons to be learned. Use these insights to improve your skills, knowledge, and decision-making in future endeavors.
- **Develop Problem-Solving Skills:** The tech industry is inherently problem-driven, so focus on honing your problem-solving skills. Break complex problems into smaller, manageable components. Use systematic approaches like root cause analysis, brainstorming, and prototyping to find innovative solutions.
- **Maintain Work-Life Balance:** Prioritize self-care and maintain a healthy work-life balance. Engage in activities outside of work that bring you joy, reduce stress, and promote physical and mental well-being. Taking breaks and disconnecting from work can recharge your energy and enhance your resilience.
- **Embrace Continuous Learning:** Stay updated with the latest trends, tools, and technologies in the tech industry. Continuously expand your knowledge and skill set through courses, workshops, conferences, and online resources. Embracing lifelong learning will keep you adaptable and resilient in the face of change.

- **Seek Feedback and Learn from Criticism:** Actively seek constructive feedback from colleagues, mentors, and supervisors. Use feedback as an opportunity for growth and improvement. Embrace criticism as a chance to refine your skills and perspective, helping you persevere and excel in your field.
- **Practice Stress Management Techniques:** Develop stress management techniques to cope with the pressures of the tech industry. Regular exercise, mindfulness meditation, deep breathing exercises, and time management strategies can help reduce stress and enhance your ability to persevere through challenging situations.

Remember, building resilience and perseverance is a continuous process. It requires patience, self-reflection, and a commitment to personal growth. By implementing these strategies and adapting them to your specific circumstances, you can cultivate the mindset and skills needed to thrive as a tech professional.

8.3 Sustainable Tech-Yoga Balance

Cultivating a sustainable yoga and tech balance for tech minds can help promote physical and mental well-being while navigating the demands of the tech industry. Here are some detailed steps to help you achieve this balance.

- **Schedule Regular Yoga Practice:** Set aside dedicated time for yoga practice in your schedule. Start with realistic goals, such as practicing twice or thrice a week, and gradually increase the frequency as you develop consistency. Consistency is critical to reaping the benefits of yoga.
- **Choose the Right Yoga Style:** Explore different yoga styles to find the one that suits your needs and preferences. Hatha yoga, Vinyasa, and Yin yoga are popular options. Hatha yoga emphasizes physical postures and breath control, Vinyasa focuses on flowing movements synchronized with breath, and Yin yoga targets deep stretching and relaxation. Experiment and find the style that resonates with you.
- **Create a Dedicated Yoga Space:** Designate a specific area in your home or workspace for yoga practice. Please keep it clean, clutter-free, and inviting. Decorate the space with calming elements such as plants, candles, or incense to enhance relaxation. Having a dedicated space helps create a ritualistic environment that encourages regular practice.
- **Start with Short Sessions:** If you have a busy schedule, begin with short yoga sessions. Even 15 minutes of practice can be beneficial. As you

become more comfortable and find time, gradually increase the duration of your sessions. Consistency is more important than the length of each session.

- **Incorporate Yoga into Breaks:** Instead of scrolling through your phone during short breaks, use that time to engage in brief yoga practices. Perform a few stretches, deep breathing exercises, or mini-meditation to recharge your energy and refresh your mind. These mini-yoga sessions throughout the day can help counteract the effects of prolonged sitting and screen time.

- **Practice Mindfulness in Tech Usage:** Be mindful of your technology usage patterns. Set boundaries and establish tech-free zones or tech-free periods during the day. Avoid checking emails or using screens right before bed to promote better sleep. Engaging in tech detoxes periodically, such as taking weekends off from screens, can also help you recharge and reconnect with yourself.

- **Use Yoga Apps and Online Resources:** Leverage technology to support your yoga practice. Numerous yoga apps, online classes, and tutorials can guide you through yoga sessions. Use them to enhance your knowledge, gain inspiration, and maintain your practice even when time or resources are limited.

- **Attend Yoga Workshops and Retreats:** Consider attending yoga workshops or retreats to deepen your practice and immerse yourself in a yoga-focused environment. These experiences can provide a break from the tech world, allow you to connect with like-minded individuals, and provide an opportunity for self-reflection and rejuvenation.
- **Practice Yoga for Stress Management:** The tech industry can be demanding and stressful. Use yoga as a tool for stress management. Incorporate relaxation techniques, such as deep breathing exercises, meditation, and restorative yoga, into your practice. These practices can help reduce stress, improve focus, and promote well-being.
- **Seek Community and Support:** Connect with a yoga community or find a yoga buddy who shares your interest in finding the balance between yoga and tech. Join local yoga studios, participate in group classes, or engage in online communities where you can share experiences, gain support, and learn from others' journeys.

Remember, the key is to find a balance that works for you. Be flexible and adapt your yoga practice to fit your lifestyle and schedule. Integrating yoga into your tech-driven life can cultivate a sustainable balance that promotes physical health, mental clarity, and overall well-being.

Chapter 9: Conclusion

Technology is a powerful tool that has revolutionized how we live, work, and connect with the world. Yet, amidst the rapid advancements and digital frenzy, it is all too easy for tech minds to feel overwhelmed, disconnected, and burnt out. As the renowned philosopher Alan Watts once said, *'The only way to make sense of change is to plunge into it, move with it, and join the dance.'* In the dance between the ancient wisdom of yoga and the fast-paced realm of technology, we have discovered a harmonious balance that can transform the lives of tech professionals.

Meet Sarah, a brilliant software engineer consumed by her job's relentless demands. Long hours hunched over a computer screen, tight deadlines, and constant pressure to deliver innovation had taken a toll on her physical and mental well-being. Sarah longed for something more, a way to reconnect with herself and find solace amidst the chaos. During a yoga retreat, Sarah stumbled upon yoga's transformative power. As she unrolled her mat and moved through the graceful flow of poses, she felt a profound sense of grounding, clarity, and inner peace. Yoga became her refuge, a sanctuary where she could recalibrate, recharge, and rediscover her essence amidst the fast-paced tech world.

9.1 Critical Ideas and Methods

The challenges tech professionals face are addressed in the book "Yoga Flow for Tech Minds," yoga is presented as a solution for promoting overall well-being. The book emphasizes the importance of work-life balance, stress management, and mindfulness.

- The foundations of yoga, including the Eight Limbs of Yoga, are introduced, focusing on self-discipline, physical postures, breath control, and meditation. The book provides specific yoga asanas to target common physical issues experienced by tech professionals, such as poor posture and neck/shoulder tension.
- Pranayama, the practice of breath control, is explored to manage stress, increase energy, and enhance mental clarity. Mindfulness and meditation techniques are introduced to improve focus, reduce stress, and cultivate presence in everyday life.
- The book highlights the practice of Yoga Nidra for deep relaxation and rejuvenation. It also explores the connection between yoga and mental well-being, offering practices and poses to reduce anxiety, enhance focus, and cultivate emotional balance.

- Strategies for building a sustainable yoga practice include setting achievable goals, maintaining consistency, and integrating yoga into daily routines. The importance of building a supportive yoga community is emphasized, with suggestions for connecting with like-minded individuals and seeking support.

Overall, "Yoga Flow for Tech Minds" offers a comprehensive approach to incorporating yoga into the lives of tech professionals, promoting physical health, mental well-being, and work-life balance.

9.2 Self-care and Harmony

Self-care and finding harmony are paramount for tech minds due to their unique challenges in the fast-paced and demanding tech industry. Here are the key reasons why self-care and harmony are crucial.

- **Stress management:** Tech professionals often experience high-stress levels due to demanding workloads, tight deadlines, and constant technological advancements. Engaging in self-care practices helps mitigate stress's adverse effects on mental and physical well-being. It allows individuals to recharge, relax, and cultivate a sense of inner calm, reducing the risk of burnout.

- **Physical well-being:** The sedentary nature of tech jobs, prolonged screen time, and poor ergonomic practices can lead to physical discomfort, musculoskeletal issues, and decreased overall health. Prioritizing self-care, such as regular exercise, proper ergonomics, and mindfulness of physical health, can help tech professionals maintain a healthy body and prevent long-term health issues.
- **Mental well-being:** The fast-paced and constantly evolving tech industry can affect mental health. Self-care practices like meditation, mindfulness, and self-reflection provide tech minds with tools to manage their mental well-being. They can enhance focus, clarity, and emotional balance, improving overall cognitive function and resilience.
- **Work-life balance:** The tech industry is notorious for its long working hours and blurred boundaries between work and personal life. Engaging in self-care and finding harmony allows tech professionals to establish healthy boundaries, allocate time for personal interests, and nurture relationships outside work. This balance is essential for preventing burnout, maintaining relationships, and fostering a sense of fulfillment beyond professional achievements.

- **Creativity and innovation:** Self-care and harmony are crucial in enhancing creativity and fostering innovation in tech. Taking time for self-reflection, relaxation, and pursuing diverse interests allows the mind to rest and rejuvenate. This can lead to fresh perspectives, out-of-the-box thinking, and breakthrough ideas that drive innovation in the tech industry.
- **Overall well-being and fulfillment:** Self-care and finding harmony contribute to an individual's well-being and life satisfaction. When tech professionals prioritize their self-care needs and establish a sense of balance, they experience increased happiness, fulfillment, and a sense of purpose both within and outside their professional roles.

Self-care and finding harmony are essential for tech minds to manage stress, maintain physical and mental well-being, establish a work-life balance, foster creativity, and lead personal and professionally fulfilling lives. Prioritizing self-care allows tech professionals to thrive in their careers while cultivating a sense of overall well-being and satisfaction.

9.3 Digital Lifestyle Balance

In today's digital age, where technology is deeply integrated into our lives, tech minds must embrace a balanced lifestyle. Achieving balance is essential for maintaining well-being, cultivating meaningful relationships, and finding fulfillment beyond professional success. Here are some key strategies to embrace a balanced lifestyle in the digital age.

- **Set boundaries:** Establish clear boundaries between work and personal life. Define specific times for work and leisure activities, and stick to them. Create designated spaces for work and relaxation, allowing for a clear distinction between the two.
- **Practice mindfulness:** Cultivate mindfulness daily, especially when engaging with technology. Be aware of how much time you spend on digital devices and their impact on your well-being. Practice mindful technology usage by taking breaks, setting limits, and being fully present at the moment.
- **Prioritize self-care:** Make self-care a priority. Engage in activities that promote physical, mental, and emotional well-being. Exercise regularly, practice yoga or meditation, get sufficient sleep, and nourish your body with healthy food. Set aside time for hobbies and interests and spend quality time with loved ones.

- **Seek human connection:** Foster meaningful connections beyond the digital realm. Engage in face-to-face interactions, have conversations, and participate in social activities. Building solid relationships provides support, connection, and a sense of belonging, which is vital for a balanced lifestyle.
- **Disconnect regularly:** Take intentional breaks from technology to recharge and rejuvenate. Engage in activities that don't involve screens, such as walking in nature, reading physical books, or pursuing hobbies. Disconnecting allows mental clarity, creativity, and an opportunity to be fully present in the offline world.
- **Reflect and reassess:** Regularly reflect on your priorities, values, and goals. Assess whether your current lifestyle aligns with what truly matters to you. Make necessary adjustments and realign your choices and actions with your core values. Regular reflection helps maintain a sense of purpose and ensures you're living in alignment with your authentic self.
- **Cultivate a supportive community:** Surround yourself with like-minded individuals prioritizing balance and well-being. Seek out communities, both online and offline, that promote healthy

lifestyles and provide support. Engage in discussions, share experiences, and learn from others' journeys.

Remember, achieving a balanced lifestyle is an ongoing process that requires conscious effort and self-reflection. Embracing a balanced lifestyle in the digital age allows tech minds to thrive personally and professionally, fostering well-being, fulfillment, and a sense of harmony in all aspects of life.

Integrating these strategies into your daily life allows you to navigate the digital age with mindfulness, create a sustainable balance between technology and well-being, and lead a more fulfilling and balanced life as a tech professional.

Appendix: Resources for Tech-Minded Yogis

In today's fast-paced world of technology, tech-minded individuals must find moments of balance and connection amidst the digital chaos. <u>Steve Jobs</u> once said, *'It's technology married with liberal arts, married with the humanities, that yields us the result that makes our hearts sing.'* This sentiment resonates deeply with tech professionals who seek to harmonize their passion for innovation with a mindful approach to life.

Tech-savvy yogis might draw inspiration from a prominent IT personality. A bright software developer, Mark spent hours absorbed in code, chasing deadlines, and seeking technical breakthroughs. Screens, algorithms, and complicated problem-solving were Mark's life. He excelled at his job but saw its toll on his body and mind.

One day, during a particularly intense period at work, Mark stumbled upon a yoga class in his office building's wellness center. Intrigued, he decided to try it, hoping it would offer a temporary respite from the relentless demands of his job. Little did he know that this single decision would transform his approach to work and his entire perspective on life.

As Mark stepped onto the mat and followed the instructor's gentle guidance, he experienced a newfound sense of presence and calm. His breath's rhythmic flow synchronized with his body's fluid movements, grounding him in the present moment. For that hour, he detached from the screens, the deadlines, and the constant stream of notifications.

In the following weeks, Mark dedicated himself to integrating yoga into his daily routine. He explored the depths of his practice, discovering the profound benefits it offered beyond physical flexibility. Yoga became his sanctuary—an oasis of tranquility amidst the tech storm. It helped him develop focus, clarity, and resilience, enabling him to navigate his work challenges with a newfound sense of ease.

His transformation inspired Mark to explore how technology could enhance his yoga practice. He delved into yoga apps, wearable devices, and online communities that allowed him to connect with fellow tech-minded yogis across the globe. Mark realized that the fusion of technology and mindfulness could amplify the benefits of both disciplines, facilitating a more holistic approach to his well-being.

Motivated by his journey, Mark compiled a comprehensive list of resources for tech-minded yogis. In this appendix, you will find a curated selection of yoga apps, mindfulness tools, wearable devices, online classes, virtual reality experiences, websites, blogs, YouTube channels, and social media communities. These resources are designed to support and inspire individuals like Mark, who seek to integrate their passion for technology with the transformative power of yoga.

Remember, dear tech-minded yogi, as you embark on this journey of balance and self-discovery, may you find harmony in the convergence of technology and mindfulness, and may your heart sing with the beauty of this union.

Namaste.

A. Recommended books and articles

Here are some recommended books and articles for tech-minded individuals interested in exploring mindfulness, personal growth, and the intersection of technology and well-being.

Books

1. "The Code of the Extraordinary Mind: 10 Unconventional Laws to Redefine Your Life and Succeed on Your Terms" by Vishen Lakhiani
2. "The Mindful Leader: 7 Practices for Transforming Your Leadership, Your Organization and Your Life" by Michael Carroll
3. "Reboot: Leadership and the Art of Growing Up" by Jerry Colonna
4. "The Tech Whisperer: On Digital Transformation and the Technologies that Enable It" by Jaspreet Bindra
5. "Rest: Why You Get More Done When You Work Less" by Alex Soojung-Kim Pang
6. "Wings of Fire: An Autobiography" by Dr. A.P.J. Abdul Kalam
7. "The Alchemist of the East: The Man Who Transformed the Lives of Abdul Kalam and Millions of Others" by Rashmi Bansal
8. "Geek Nation: How Indian Science is Taking Over the World" by Angela Saini

9. "Wired to Care: How Companies Prosper When They Create Widespread Empathy" by Dev Patnaik
10. "India Connected: How the Smartphone Is Transforming the World's Largest Democracy" by Ravi Agrawal
11. "Digital Minimalism: Choosing a Focused Life in a Noisy World" by Cal Newport
12. "The Mind Illuminated: A Complete Meditation Guide Integrating Buddhist Wisdom and Brain Science" by Culadasa (John Yates) and Matthew Immergut
13. "10% Happier: How I Tamed the Voice in My Head, Reduced Stress Without Losing My Edge, and Found Self-Help That Works" by Dan Harris
14. "The Attention Merchants: The Epic Scramble to Get Inside Our Heads" by Tim Wu
15. "Altered Traits: Science Reveals How Meditation Changes Your Mind, Brain, and Body" by Daniel Goleman and Richard J. Davidson
16. "The Power of Now: A Guide to Spiritual Enlightenment" by Eckhart Tolle "The Shallows: What the Internet Is Doing to Our Brains" by Nicholas Carr
17. "Sapiens: A Brief History of Humankind" by Yuval Noah Harari
18. "The Four Agreements: A Practical Guide to Personal Freedom" by Don Miguel Ruiz

19. "The Art of Stillness: Adventures in Going Nowhere" by Pico Iyer

Articles

1. "The Mindful Revolution" by Hariprasad Chaurasia (published in Forbes India)
2. "The Power of Mindful Leadership" by Prabhu Guptara (published in Business Today)
3. "Digital India: The Implications of an Ambitious Initiative" by Nandan Nilekani (published in Harvard Business Review)
4. "Technology and Mindfulness: The Secret to a Balanced Life" by Rohit Talwar (published in Outlook Business)
5. "The Internet of Things and its Impact on Business and Society" by Sanjay Puri (published in Entrepreneur India)
6. "Innovation and the Indian Mindset" by R. Gopalakrishnan (published in Harvard Business Review)
7. "Can India be a World-Leading Tech Innovator?" by Nilofer Merchant (published in Harvard Business Review)
8. "Mindfulness: The Path to a Digital Detox" by Rajeev Kurapati (published in YourStory)

9. "Navigating the Challenges of Technology Addiction" by Manish Srivastava (published in The Economic Times)
10. "The Future of Work: Digital Transformation and Its Impact on Jobs in India" by Kunal Sen (published in India Today)
11. "The Science of Mindfulness" by Ronald D. Siegel (published in Psychology Today)
12. "How to Practice Mindfulness Throughout Your Work Day" by Rasmus Hougaard and Jacqueline Carter (published in Harvard Business Review)
13. "The Impact of Technology on Well-Being" by Adam Alter (published in Scientific American)
14. "Digital Detox: The Beauty of Boredom" by Manoush Zomorodi (published on TED Ideas)
15. "The Attention Economy and the Net" by Michael H. Goldhaber (published in First Monday)
16. "The Future of Happiness: 5 Modern Strategies for Balancing Productivity and Well-Being" by Amy Blankson (published on Positive Psychology Program)
17. "How Technology Is Changing the Practice and Science of Mindfulness" by Jason Farman (published in Mindful)
18. "The Mindful Revolution" by Kate Pickert (published in Time Magazine)

19. "The Dark Side of Wearable Technology" by Kate Lister (published in The Guardian)
20. "Why We Should Embrace the Slow Internet Movement" by Jennifer R. Whitson (published on The Conversation)

These books and articles provide valuable insights into the impact of technology on our well-being, practical tips for incorporating mindfulness into our daily lives, and a broader understanding of the digital landscape we navigate. They offer diverse perspectives and thought-provoking ideas to help tech-minded individuals navigate the digital age while nurturing their personal growth and overall well-being.

B. Yoga apps and online platforms

Some top yoga apps and online platforms are widely recognized and trusted by tech-minded individuals.

1. **Sarva:** Sarva is an Indian yoga and wellness startup that offers live and on-demand yoga classes through its app. They provide a variety of yoga styles, meditation sessions, and wellness programs. Sarva blends modern technology with traditional yoga practices to make yoga accessible and engaging.
2. **Aayu:** Aayu is an app designed to promote holistic well-being, offering yoga, meditation, and fitness classes. They provide diverse yoga practices taught by experienced instructors and features such as personalized recommendations, progress tracking, and social sharing.
3. **Yoga Studio:** as mentioned earlier, Yoga Studio is a widely recognized app that offers a comprehensive library of yoga classes for all levels. It provides HD video classes, customizable programs, and the ability to create your classes. The app caters to the needs of tech-minded individuals in India as well.
4. **Art of Living Yoga:** The Art of Living Yoga app was developed by the Art of Living Foundation and was founded by Sri Sri Sri Shankar. It offers a

collection of yoga practices, guided meditation, and breathing exercises. The app also includes spiritual talks, wellness tips, and features to track your progress.

5. **YogaGlo:** YogaGlo, as mentioned earlier, is an online platform that offers a wide range of yoga classes taught by experienced instructors. Their platform is accessible in India and provides diverse styles and practices suitable for tech-minded individuals.

6. **Yoga Studio:** This app offers a vast library of yoga classes for all levels, from beginner to advanced. It provides HD video classes, customizable programs, and the ability to create your classes. The app also includes options for meditation and relaxation.

7. **Down Dog**: Down Dog is a highly-rated app that provides a variety of yoga classes, including vinyasa, hatha, restorative, and more. It offers customizable practices based on your level, time availability, and specific focus areas. The app also provides options for music and voice guidance.

8. **Glo:** Glo is an online platform that offers yoga, meditation, and Pilates classes taught by renowned instructors. It provides a wide range of styles, durations, and levels, ensuring there's something for everyone. Glo also features programs and challenges to help you deepen your practice.

9. **YogaGlo:** YogaGlo offers a vast library of online yoga classes for all levels, including various styles and durations. The platform allows you to search for classes based on your needs and preferences. YogaGlo also provides specialized programs and courses taught by experienced instructors.
10. **Yoga International:** Yoga International provides access to many yoga classes, workshops, and articles. It offers diverse yoga styles and practices, including therapeutic, Yin, and meditation. The platform also features programs and challenges to support your growth.
11. **Gaia:** Gaia is an online streaming platform that offers a wide range of yoga classes, documentaries, and shows on topics related to yoga, mindfulness, and personal growth. It includes classes for all levels and styles and content on nutrition, spirituality, and holistic well-being.
12. **Daily Yoga**: Daily Yoga is a popular app that provides guided yoga classes, workout plans, and meditation sessions. It offers various programs and challenges tailored to specific goals and preferences. The app also includes a pose library, community support, and integration with wearable devices.
13. **Alo Moves:** Alo Moves is an online platform that offers yoga, fitness, and meditation classes taught

by world-class instructors. It provides a diverse range of styles, from vinyasa flow to power yoga and yin yoga. Alo Moves also features curated programs and challenges for different needs.

Remember to explore these apps and online platforms to find the one that aligns with your preferences, goals, and level of expertise. These platforms offer a wealth of resources and classes to support your yoga practice, regardless of your tech-savvy nature.

C. Yoga studios and retreats with a tech focus

While yoga studios and retreats with a specific tech focus may be relatively limited, several yoga studios and retreat centers cater to tech-minded individuals by offering a harmonious blend of technology and mindfulness. Here are a few notable ones.

1. **Rishikesh Yog Peeth (Rishikesh, Uttarakhand):** Rishikesh Yog Peeth is a well-known yoga school in Rishikesh, often called the "Yoga Capital of the World." They offer a variety of yoga teacher training programs, workshops, and retreats that focus on traditional yogic practices while addressing the challenges of modern technology.

2. **Art of Living International Center (Bengaluru, Karnataka):** The Art of Living International Center is a renowned spiritual and wellness retreat founded by Sri Sri Ravi Shankar. Alongside meditation and mindfulness programs, they occasionally organize workshops and events that explore the impact of technology on well-being and offer practical tools to find balance.

3. **Sivananda Yoga Vedanta Dhanwantari Ashram (Neyyar Dam, Kerala):** The Sivananda Ashram in Neyyar Dam is an authentic yoga ashram that offers residential yoga retreats,

courses, and workshops. They emphasize classical yoga practices, including asanas, pranayama, meditation, and philosophy, providing a serene environment for self-reflection and mindfulness.

4. **Parmarth Niketan (Rishikesh, Uttarakhand):** Parmarth Niketan is a renowned ashram on the Ganges River banks in Rishikesh. While their primary focus is on traditional spiritual practices, they occasionally host workshops and events that address the challenges of the digital age and explore the integration of technology and mindfulness.

5. **Isha Yoga Center (Coimbatore, Tamil Nadu):** The Isha Yoga Center, founded by Sadhguru Jaggi Vasudev, offers a variety of yoga programs and retreats that emphasize inner transformation and well-being. While not exclusively focused on technology, their teachings often touch upon finding balance in the modern world and utilizing technology mindfully.

6. **The Yoga Barn (Ubud, Bali):** The Yoga Barn is a renowned yoga studio and retreat center that hosts workshops, classes, and retreats in the heart of Bali. They occasionally offer specialized programs focused on the intersection of mindfulness, spirituality, and technology, exploring how to find balance in the digital age.

7. **Esalen Institute (Big Sur, California):** Esalen Institute is a retreat center that offers a wide range of workshops and programs focused on personal growth, spirituality, and well-being. They often host retreats that explore the impact of technology on our lives and provide tools for finding balance through practices like yoga, meditation, and contemplation.
8. **Breathing Space (London, UK):** Breathing Space is a yoga studio in London that offers classes and workshops emphasizing the relationship between mindfulness, technology, and well-being. They explore how yoga and mindfulness practices can help navigate the digital world with more significant presence and intention.
9. **Yoga Vida (New York City, USA):** Yoga Vida is a famous yoga studio in New York City that provides classes, workshops, and events designed for the urban lifestyle. While not exclusively focused on technology, they often incorporate discussions on mindfulness in the digital age, encouraging tech-minded individuals to find balance through their practice.
10. **Spirit Rock Meditation Center (Woodacre, California):** Spirit Rock is a meditation center that offers retreats and programs focused on mindfulness, meditation, and contemplative

practices. While not explicitly tech-focused, they occasionally host retreats exploring the intersection of technology, mindfulness, and the modern world.

11. **The Shambhala Mountain Center (Red Feather Lakes, Colorado):** The Shambhala Mountain Center is a retreat center nestled in the Rocky Mountains that offers a variety of meditation retreats, including programs that explore the impact of technology on our lives. They provide a serene environment to unplug and reconnect with oneself.

These studios and retreat centers may focus on more than just technology. Still, they often incorporate discussions, workshops, and programs that address the challenges and opportunities tech-minded individuals face in their quest for balance, mindfulness, and personal growth. Check their schedules and offerings to find specific programs that align with your interests and goals.

Acknowledgment

I want to express my deepest gratitude to my family and friends who have unwavering support throughout the creation of "Yoga Flow for Tech Minds: Cultivating Balance and Wellness in the Digital Age." Your constant love, encouragement, and unwavering faith in me have been the driving force behind this book. I am grateful for your presence, cheers, and reminders to maintain a balanced mindset.

To my mentors, coaches, and author friends, I am immensely thankful for your guidance, wisdom, and profound influence on my personal growth. Your unwavering belief in my abilities and invaluable insights have played a significant role in my journey toward success. I highly regard the lessons you have taught me and your positive impact on my life.

I extend my heartfelt gratitude to all the readers and supporters of my work. Your enthusiasm, feedback, and encouragement have been a constant source of inspiration. Your belief in the power of cultivating balance and wellness in the digital age fuels my determination to continue spreading this vital message. Thank you for embracing "Yoga Flow for Tech Minds" and joining me on this transformative journey.

Finally, I thank everyone who helped bring this book to existence. From the committed scholars and experts whose work I have leaned upon to the individuals who freely offered their experiences and viewpoints, your united efforts have considerably expanded the substance and deepened the overall significance of this book. Your contributions are much appreciated.

Thank you all for being part of this incredible journey.

About the Author

The author of "Yoga Flow for Tech Minds," with a remarkable career spanning over three decades in corporate and government IT enterprises, brings a wealth of experience. A true embodiment of versatility, he excelled in the tech industry and pursued a passion for yoga and Ayurvedic life management. As a dedicated yoga instructor and practitioner, he understands the unique challenges faced by tech minds in the digital age.

Born on August 26, 1968, in the serene hamlet of Pulgaon, Maharashtra's Wardha district, the author's journey has been continuous growth and learning. Completing his Higher Secondary School education in Hindi medium from Ordinance Factory Higher Secondary School Katni, Madhya Pradesh, in 1984, he earned an Engineering degree from Government Engineering College Jabalpur in 1990. With an unwavering commitment to personal development, he also pursued a part-time MBA in 2010.

Beyond technology and yoga, the author finds solace and inspiration in various pursuits. An ardent lover of music, movies, and motivational books, he finds fulfillment in exploring new destinations and volunteering in Nagpur, famously known as Orange City.

With a profound belief in the power of perseverance, the author views obstacles as stepping stones to success. He understands that accurate achievement results from unwavering dedication and strenuous effort. As a member of the Toastmasters club, he has honed his communication and leadership skills, further enriching his ability to inspire and empower others.

Through "Yoga Flow for Tech Minds," the author shares his unique blend of expertise in the tech industry, yoga, and personal growth. Drawing on his diverse background and unwavering commitment to well-being, he offers practical insights and transformative practices to help tech minds find balance, overcome challenges, and reach their full potential.

Join the author on this empowering journey of self-discovery and transformation. Learn from his experiences, embrace the opportunities that arise from obstacles, and embark on a path of holistic well-being in the digital age.

Can you do me a favor?

Dear Readers,

First and foremost, I want to extend my deepest gratitude to you for choosing to embark on this transformative journey with me through the pages of "Yoga Flow for Tech Minds: Cultivating Balance and Wellness in the Digital Age." Your decision to invest your time and attention in this book is truly invaluable.

I worked hard on this book to encourage and inspire you to discover balance and well-being in the digital era. Today, I have a modest request.

If you find value in the ideas, strategies, and stories shared within these chapters, I kindly ask for your support in spreading the word. Your positive experiences and recommendations can make a significant impact by reaching and touching the lives of more individuals.

In this digital era, your voice holds immense influence. By leaving reviews on platforms like Amazon, Goodreads, or any other platform where you feel comfortable, you can help others discover the transformative power of "Yoga Flow for Tech Minds: Cultivating Balance and Wellness in the Digital Age." Your genuine thoughts and feedback will guide potential readers, empowering them to make informed decisions and embark on their personal and professional growth journey.

Furthermore, if you resonate with the message of this book and would like to connect further, I invite you to engage with me on social media platforms such as Facebook, LinkedIn, and Instagram. Together, let us build a community of like-minded individuals passionate about embracing their potential, supporting one another, and celebrating each other's victories.

Please remember that success is not solely an individual pursuit but a collective endeavor. Together, we can create a ripple effect that spreads positivity, motivation, and a wellness-centered mindset to every corner of the world.

Once again, I express my heartfelt gratitude for joining me on this transformative journey. Your support and assistance in sharing "Yoga Flow for Tech Minds: Cultivating Balance and Wellness in the Digital Age" would mean the world to me. Together, let's inspire and empower others to find harmony and well-being in the fast-paced world of technology.

With profound appreciation,

DILIP PATIL

Discover More

Dear Readers,

As you begin your powerful journey through "Yoga Flow for Tech Minds: Cultivating Balance and Wellness in the Digital Age," I want to offer some of my prior works on personal growth, success, and self-mastery. Each book explores the human potential and gives practical advice to help you succeed.

My prior efforts include the following.

1. **"Empowering Yourself to Achieve Success"**: This book explores personal growth and the keys to reaching your most significant potential. It guides you through problems, challenges, and objectives with powerful thinking adjustments, practical solutions, and inspiring tales.

2. **"The Path to Lasting Happiness:** Unveiling the Key to Creating an Abundant and Purposeful Life" covers Purpose & Values, Mindset, Relationships, Gratitude and Mindfulness, Resilience, Stress Management, Self-care, Sustainable Planning, Career and Balance, and Science. It discusses communication styles, active listening, and empathy-building. Communication skills help you connect, influence, and work with people, leading to success in all aspects of life.

3. **"The Success Mindset:** Think Like a Winner," my first book in "THE ART OF SUCCESS." This book helps you reach your potential and succeed. It draws on years of research, personal experiences, and the best minds from many areas. Discover how a winning attitude may change your life in these pages.

I welcome you to examine these prior works if they interest you. Each book, like "Yoga Flow for Tech Minds," offers personal and professional growth opportunities with enthusiasm and devotion.

Visit **www.patildilip.com** or **Amazon** to discover and buy more about each book (www.amazon.com). These books will inspire, empower, and equip you to succeed in all areas of life.

Thank you for supporting this transformational journey.

With thanks,

DILIP PATIL

Printed in Great Britain
by Amazon